EBURY PRESS
TEACHINGS FROM THE RAMAYANA

Shantanu Gupta is the founder of The Vedic IQ and The Ramayana School, where he teaches life lessons from the Ramayana and other Indian scriptures to families across the globe. Shantanu has held workshops on life lessons from the Ramayana for thousands of participants across twenty-plus countries. Shantanu is also a part-time faculty at the Hindu University of America, Florida, where he teaches the Ramayana.

He is also the biographer of Uttar Pradesh chief minister Yogi Adityanath, with his three books titled *The Monk Who Became Chief Minister*, *The Monk Who Transformed Uttar Pradesh* and *Ajay to Yogi Adityanath*. Shantanu has done his engineering from GB Pant University, his management studies from XLRI, Jamshedpur, and his policy studies from the University of Sussex, UK. He is a Chevening Gurukul fellow from the University of Oxford.

T0158263

teachings from the

RAMAYANA

~~on~~

FAMILY & LIFE

Shantanu Gupta

EBURY
PRESS

An imprint of Penguin Random House

EBURY PRESS

USA | Canada | UK | Ireland | Australia
New Zealand | India | South Africa | China | Singapore

Ebury Press is part of the Penguin Random House group of companies
whose addresses can be found at global.penguinrandomhouse.com

Published by Penguin Random House India Pvt. Ltd
4th Floor, Capital Tower 1, MG Road,
Gurugram 122 002, Haryana, India

First published in Ebury Press by Penguin Random House India 2023

10 9 8 7 6 5 4 3

ISBN 9780143461463

Typeset in Sabon by Manipal Technologies Limited, Manipal
Printed at Replika Press Pvt. Ltd, India

www.penguin.co.in

Contents

Part III
Aranya Kanda
Bad Choices Lead to Bad Outcomes

Part IV
Kishkinda Kanda
Value of Strategic Partnership in Life

Part V
Sundar Kanda
Value of Trust and Judgement

Part VI
Yudha Kanda
Don't Be Surrounded by Yes-Men

Preface

I am a huge enthusiast of the Ramayana.* My extensive research of the epic offered me the perspectives that compelled me to understand and explore its potential to bring palpable positive changes in our lives. The year I decided to begin a school based on the teachings of the Ramayana, the pandemic hit us. Nevertheless, I rolled out The Ramayana School, which received a good response. This encouraged me to look for life lessons and leadership from this Indian odyssey and its characters, to organize learning modules for general readers, children and young adults.

While our education system continues to focus on utilitarian learning emphasizing the importance of edtech apps to teach maths, science and coding, among other subjects, I felt the need for value-based education, which could throw light on the idea of resilience, honesty,

---

* Valmiki's Ramayana, www.valmiki.iitk.ac.in, and Tulsi's Ramayana (*Ramcharitmanas*).

kindness, compassion, truthfulness and the skills to resolve conflicts and manage constant stress, which contemporary society burdens us with every moment. We seldom come across a system that helps us understand and imbibe the art of robust decision-making. The lifelong chase for a higher intelligence quotient (IQ) alone keeps us and our families poor in emotional quotient (EQ). A high IQ might keep us ahead in our career race, but a low EQ has the potential to make us lose in many other challenges that modern life throws at us.

Even if you are a super-smart coder, a brilliant scientist, a top-notch business tycoon or a world-renowned doctor, life will not stop posing complicated emotional challenges to you. Are we preparing our families to adequately deal with such situations?

This book is an endeavour to explore and contextualize the life lessons hidden in the Ramayana essentially for families. It attempts to dive deep into the stories, conversations and characters of the Ramayana, and to translate them into real-life learnings for a happy family.

Rama spent fourteen years, driven by his grit and determination, in exile. In those fourteen years, he faced the worst of the challenges that one can possibly face in one's life. He was about to become the king of the mighty Kosala kingdom, but instead, he was sentenced to exile. When, despite all the hardships, he completed almost thirteen years of exile, his wife was kidnapped. He had to fight a life-threatening war with the mighty army of Ravana. During those fourteen years, he almost lost his kingdom, almost lost his wife and almost lost his life. But despite all that, he did not take any shortcuts, he did not run back to his brother Bharata for assistance, he did not lose his honesty, his goodness, his righteousness. And he finally won the war against Ravana.

After the initial agony of his wife's kidnapping, he calmed himself. He used all the skills he had learnt from various teachers in his life. He strategized based on whatever resources were available to him. He made local allies in the form of Hanuman, Sugriva and their teams. Hanuman helped him in his search for Sita; Angada helped him in his diplomatic peace mission; Jambavan helped him to keep the team motivated; the engineers Nala and Neel helped him to make the Rama Bridge to cross the sea to Lanka; Vibhishana helped him to penetrate through the secrets of the opposition army. In the end, Rama and his *vanara** army won against the mighty Ravana and his resourceful, well-equipped army. Rama's sheer perseverance won over the might of Ravana.

We have made plenty of decisions since childhood, both mundane and critically important ones. From what to wear today to what to eat, which course to study, which college to take admission in, whether to marry, whom to marry, which company to work for, which area to work in, how to respond to a happy situation, how to respond to an ugly situation, how to treat a friend, etc. Our decision-making is put to work at various moments. What we decide and what we choose at crucial moments in our life journey shape our lives. In the Ramayana, there are various

---

* Vanara: Vana + Nara. It refers to the people living in the jungle.

characters who made very wise choices from the options available to them, and there are some who made a wrong choice—we can learn profoundly from both and develop our own robust decision-making framework for life.

In this book, I would like to narrate the story of the Ramayana chronologically, in the form of twenty-five substories. Each substory will drive a quintessential life lesson, which you can imbibe and share with your family. In each of these twenty-five segments, we will also take a pause and engage with a real-time family scenario, with multiple possible options and recommendations for the family, drawn from the Ramayana—steps that all members of the family can practise. I will also be using some non-translatable Sanskrit words in this book directly and will explain their wider meaning in English in the footnotes.

Consider this book as your personal engagement with the Ramayana. I have created sections for you to take notes and have put together critical-thinking questions after each life lesson, for the whole family to ponder, and reflection sections to explore your own Rama and Ravana qualities. We also have a crossword puzzle at the end of each Kanda to help you revise names of all the places and characters. I invite you all to engage with this book and see if you can treat it as a life-skills course for the entire family.

PART I

Bala Kanda[*]
Importance of a Good Teacher in Life

---

[*] *Kanda* means a part or a section of the Ramayana.

1

Develop Expertise like Rishi[*] Rishyasringa

Ayodhya, the capital of the kingdom of Kosala, was prosperous, healthy and well fortified. (Ayodhya lies in today's Uttar Pradesh.) Its army was known for its valour. The citizens of Ayodhya were committed to its development and had great respect for their meritorious kings. King Dasharatha was happy to see his kingdom's prosperity and his citizens' progress. But he was constantly thinking of Ayodhya's future: Who will take care of his beloved Ayodhya after him? And to whom will he give the reins of his kingdom after him?

The king's constant grief alerted his adviser Rishi Vasishtha, who suggested that the king perform the 'Putr Kamesthi Yagna', for childbearing. Rishi Vasishtha told

---

[*] Rishi means a saint, hermit or monk.

the king that it was the most powerful yagna* performed for the purpose. Rishi Vasishtha also added that it was a tough ritual and that only a few experts could perform it with the utmost sanctity. He advised the king that Rishi Rishyasringa was one of the few capable ones to perform this yagna with precision. Rishi Rishyasringa was indeed one of the most famous scholars of his time and was known for his expertise. All the great kings and renowned sages valued his work, had great respect for him and lauded him with honours. Rishi Rishyasringa used to live and practise his craft away from the kingdoms in a remote hermitage. Now, the challenge was to reach out to the expert and convince him to perform the yagna in Ayodhya.

Knowledge and expertise were worshiped and revered in those times. So much so that the mighty king Dasharatha decided to visit the sage himself to invite him to Ayodhya. King Dasharatha went to Rishi Rishyasringa's ashram in the dense woods without the soldiers and guards of his most powerful Chaturangini Sena,† without his

---

* *Yagna* or *Yajna* is a Sanskrit word which refers to the Vedic ritual done in front of a sacred fire, with mantras and offerings made of different combinations of herbs as sacrifice into the fire to attain different spiritual goals.

† Chaturangini Sena of Dasharatha was his famous and powerful four-pronged army.

illustrious crown, without his grand chariot, even without his footwear. The rare expertise of the sage had made King Dasharatha reach out to him without any kingly protocols. Rishis were rational people. Rishi Rishyasringa heard Dasharatha's genuine problem and agreed to perform the yagna in Ayodhya.

Soon, the preparations for the yagna began. Dasharatha invited the kings from all over the surrounding regions. As Rishi Rishyasringa began the yagna, the entire place was filled with the positive vibrations of Vedic chants. After a couple of hours of rigorous chanting and pouring of selected sacrificial herbs by Rishi Rishyasringa, a majestic human form emerged from the blazing fire: the 'Yagna Purush'. Yagna Purush* gave a bowl of kheer (rice pudding) to King Dasharatha.

* Yagna Purush refers to the divine being who appeared as the result of the powerful yagna.

Dasharatha distributed the sacred food among his three wives: Kausalya, Kaikeyi and Sumitra. And soon, the auspicious day came when Queen Kausalya gave birth to Rama, Queen Kaikeyi gave birth to Bharata and Queen Sumitra gave birth to twins, Laxmana and Shatrughna. The whole city was filled with joy and celebrations. The king distributed jewels, grains and valuable gems among the Brahmins and villagers. The entire city of Ayodhya was decorated with the choicest of flowers. Every citizen celebrated the arrival of the four princes in their own way.

Life Lesson #1 for Families

The great king Dasharatha himself went to the woods to get the expert Rishi Rishyasringa to Ayodhya. The king went barefoot, without his crown, without his army, in honour of the sage, to convince and request him to perform the grand prayer 'Putr Kamesthi Yagna'.

Every family can learn two important things from King Dasharatha's action. First, that every progressive society should value, revere and respect its experts for their knowledge and for the hard work they had put in to gain that knowledge. Second, that we should help each member of the family, especially the children, to develop an expertise, be useful to society and become a well-respected member of the community. Rishi Rishyasringa has taught us that:

> Experts are valued even by kings. So,
> develop expertise.

Family Scenario #1

For any family, the future of the children of that family is quite important. Based on parents, teachers, friends and other influences around, children make their career goals. Many career goals are based on popular choices, like becoming an engineer or a doctor. As a parent, how do you want to orient your children's choices for career?

A) I just want my child to be a highly paid professional in some multinational company
B) I want my child to explore career options according to his or her passion
C) I want my child to be an expert in his or her field, someone respected for his or her knowledge

Guidance for Families from the Ramayana #1

Becoming an expert on a topic or a subject requires nothing less than a *tapasya.* Our ancient scientists or rishis used to practise the same. Apart from helping you become an expert, tapasya also makes you self-disciplined and a lifelong seeker of more knowledge. An expert is always valued by society. We have seen how the powerful king Dasharatha valued the expertise of Rishi Rishyasringa. As per various child development theories, human beings are

---

* Tapasya is a Sanskrit word which means deep meditation, self-discipline and efforts to attain knowledge.

governed with multiple forms of intelligence. Hence, every child is naturally and especially talented and interested in one or two types of unique intelligence, which may differ from their parents' criteria or preferences. Support your child in identifying and developing that special talent, and utilize that particular aspect of intelligence as you learn to allow your child to gain expertise.

Family Reflection Time

Document your reflections from the Rishi Rishyasringa episode. Do you want to be an expert like Rishi Rishyasringa or a generalist? You may want to jot down your reflections, click a picture and share on social media with the hashtag **#MyRamayana**.

_____

_____

_____

_____

_____

_____

_____

_____

_____

Idiom and Phrases from the Ramayana

Make your sentences using 'Rishi Rishyasringa' instead of the word 'expert'.

Example: At Google's Bengaluru office, Arjun is considered a **Rishi Rishyasringa** of search engine algorithms.

_____

_____

_____

_____

_____

_____

_____

_____

_____

_____

_____

_____

_____

_____

2

Have Long-Term Vision like Rishi Vasishtha

All the four princes, Rama, Laxmana, Bharata and Shatrughna, were growing up fast. The growing-up years of Rama and his beloved brothers were the most cherishable moments for King Dasharatha and the three queens. All the four brothers shared a special bond of love and respect for each other. King Dasharatha was extremely contented to see the brotherhood and harmony among his sons. All the princes were very fortunate to get trained under the guidance of Sage Vasishtha, in the ancient gurukul system of education. They learnt the art of archery, got well versed in the divine texts of the Vedas, learnt economics, politics, warcraft and other skills required for robust statecraft.

Dasharatha was happy to observe the upbringing of his children. But then came a testing situation. One day, Sage Vishwamitra arrived in Ayodhya. Dasharatha

felt honoured and pleased to welcome such a renowned and learned sage to his kingdom. Without even asking, Dasharatha offered Sage Vishwamitra any help under the sun. The sage shared his concern that some notorious demons were disturbing his group of saints in performing their prayers and rituals in the forests. Vishwamitra, with high hopes, asked Dasharatha to send his two sons, Rama and Laxmana, with him into the woods to eliminate those demons. Hearing this request, the king was taken aback. Dasharatha pleaded the revered sage not to ask him to send his beloved young sons into the forests to fight the powerful demons, as they were just teenagers. He suggested that the sage command him or his powerful army to fight those demons but not ask for his young, tender boys to accompany the sage.

After listening to
Dasharatha's refusal,
Vishwamitra was
outraged and filled
with the anger he
was known for. He
told the king that his
conduct was unworthy of a king of the Ikshvaku lineage.
Sage Vishwamitra further asserted that he only needed
Rama and Laxmana, and no one else. Dasharatha did
not know what to do. He was blinded by his short-term
emotions: love, care and a sense of overprotectiveness for
his sons.

At that moment, Sage Vasishtha intervened and gave
some good wisdom to the king. He told the king that his
sons were extremely fortunate to get a teacher like Sage
Vishwamitra. At the gurukul in Ayodhya, the princes had
mastered their classroom lessons. Now it was the time
for practical, on-ground training for them. With Sage
Vishwamitra, they would receive a hands-on training on
practical warfare and facing real-life challenges.

He guided the king about the long-term prospect of his
sons' education and advised him to not get bogged down by
his short-term emotions. Sage Vasishtha further explained
to King Dasharatha that Sage Vishwamitra was fully capable
of handling those demons himself. If the sage was asking for
Rama and Laxmana's help, there must be a larger purpose
hidden in it for the young boys. After much guidance and
coaching by Sage Vasishtha, King Dasharatha, with a heavy
heart, agreed to send his sons to the jungle.

Later it turned out that this journey benefitted Rama and Laxmana immensely. They received the best training and guidance, which helped them profoundly in their future.

Life Lesson #2 for Families

Rishi Vasishtha told King Dasharatha that he had given classroom training to Rama and Laxmana through gurukul education, but now they needed practical field training. Rishi Vasishtha persuaded King Dasharatha to send Rama and Laxmana with Rishi Vishwamitra, for the long-term development and training of the princes, with such a divine guru. Rishi Vasishtha has taught us:

> **Always target long-term goals, rather than think about short-term emotions and benefits.**

Family Scenario #2

Your daughter Meera is thirteen years old. Apart from doing well academically, she has shown good performance in school- and city-level badminton championships. The whole family takes pride in her achievements. Coaches see a promising talent in her. One major academy in Hyderabad is ready to train her professionally. But taking her game to the next level has its own challenges. Moreover, for the next set of badminton tournaments she has to travel to various parts of the country. And the thought of her travelling to different parts of the country at this young age can also be quite unnerving for the family. If your family faces such a situation, what will you do?

A) You will make her focus only on studies as of now
B) Along with her studies, you will let her continue her badminton practice, but at a local level
C) As per the coaches' guidance, you will make every effort possible so that she plays in the national and international circuit

Guidance for Families from the Ramayana #2

Getting access to a good teacher, a good guru, is one of the high points for any learner. Whenever you get the opportunity to learn from the right teacher, grab that opportunity with both hands. Many a time, our over protectiveness for our family members becomes detrimental to their growth. A long-term perspective on life should always outweigh short-term considerations. If Dasharatha had given in to his overprotective impulse towards his sons and not sent Rama and Laxmana with Sage Vishwamitra, the boys would have missed the profound teachings from the great teacher.

Family Reflection Time

Document Your reflections from the Sage Vishwamitra episode. Will you send your children with a great teacher for better learning? You may want to jot down your reflections, click a picture and share on social media with the hashtag **#MyRamayana**.

_____

_____

_____

_____

_____

_____

_____

_____

_____

_____

_____

Family Breakfast Discussion

If Dasharatha had not sent Rama and Laxmana with Sage Vishwamitra, how would the Ramayana storyline have differed? You may want to jot down your reflections, click a picture and share on social media with the hashtag **#MyRamayana**.

_____

_____

_____

_____

_____

_____

_____

_____

_____

_____

3

Keep Your Moral Compass on Even in Times of Crisis, like Rama Did

Rama and Laxmana left for the jungle with Sage Vishwamitra. After crossing Ayodhya, they entered the dense forest of Dandaka. Sage Vishwamitra told them that Dandaka forest had once been filled with life. Sages, animals, birds and insects, all lived happily in the jungle, before demoness Tadaka devastated this beautiful forest and turned it into a lifeless and scary place.

The jungle was dense, and the way was tough. Sage Vishwamitra narrated many historical incidents to Rama and Laxmana on their journey, to keep them  motivated and alert. He told the boys about the Samudra*

---

* Samudra means sea or ocean.

Manthan* between the Devatas and the Asuras,† from which
Amrit, the heavenly nectar of immortality, and Halahala,
the lethal poison, both emerged. He also motivated the
boys by narrating the story of their forefather Bhagirath,
who got River Ganga to earth by his hard work, dedication
and engineering acumen. These stories were not only
interesting but were also packed with factual learnings and
lessons for the young princes.

The three of them
had reached closer
to their destination.
Sage Vishwamitra
guided Rama and
Laxmana to the place
of residence of Tadaka
in the jungle. Tadaka,
who was capable of

smelling human flesh, smelt their presence and came out.
She looked ferocious. There was a vicious eagerness in her
eyes. Till then, Rama had lived comfortably and trained
in Dasharatha's palace in Ayodhya; he had practised his
archery on non-moving, non-living targets, and his warcraft
was based on artificial scenarios and case studies. This was
the first real-life crisis Rama and Laxmana were facing in
their lives. Vishwamitra asked Rama to pull the string of his
bow, point a sharp arrow towards Tadaka and eliminate her
as soon as possible.

---

* Manthan means churning of the ocean.
† Devatas refers to the good and the divine beings. Asuras refers
to the evil beings.

A dangerous crisis, in the form of Tadaka, was standing in front of Rama. Though Rama was in his teens, he was skilled and brave enough to counter a ferocious demoness like Tadaka. He pulled the string of his bow and targeted his sharpest arrow towards Tadaka. He was ready to launch the arrow at her. But at that very moment, he expressed his unwillingness to kill Tadaka, as she was a woman and Rama had been taught by his guru not to hurt any women. Though it was a critical situation, Rama's moral compass was fully active. He was capable of solving the problem, but not immorally.

Sage Vishwamitra was pleasantly surprised by Rama's moral dilemma even at the moment of crisis. Sage Vishwamitra replied to Rama that he was right about not wanting to hurt a woman. But Vishwamitra added that Tadaka only possessed the body of a woman—she did not have the feminine qualities of compassion, kindness and motherhood. She killed children, women, men and sages mercilessly. After hearing about the cruel deeds of Tadaka, Rama felt convinced and launched his arrow ferociously at Tadaka. The arrow pierced her chest, and the huge demoness fell down, lifeless. Pleased and happy with Rama's valour at this young age, Sage Vishwamitra blessed Rama with more power and gifted a set of divine weapons to him.

Life Lesson #3 for Families

Even when in crisis, Rama did not abandon his moral compass to somehow just solve the crisis unethically. Once Rama's moral dilemma was solved, only then did he go ahead and kill Tadaka. Rama has taught us that we should:

> Uphold high moral standards even in times of crisis.

Family Scenario #3

You are coming back home from a car showroom after buying a brand-new car. Your twelve-year-old child is also sitting next to you while you are driving the new car back to your house. A biker, wrongly overtaking your car from the left, bumps into your car. Your brand-new car, even before reaching the temple and the house, has received an ugly dent on the door and a broken headlight. What would your likely reaction be at the accident site?

A) You will shout and use abusive words for the biker, as it was the biker's fault
B) You will end up hitting the biker in anger, to teach him a lesson
C) You will be firm and assertive while making your point, but with politeness
D) You will leave the place, without any discussion or altercation

Guidance for Families from the Ramayana #3

In such a situation, never presume that the other person will necessarily argue or fight back. You can say: 'My car has been hit by your vehicle. How do you want to compensate? Do you have insurance?' Describe the situation factually, without using 'I' and 'you' as much as possible.

If the other person starts blaming or picking a fight, you can firmly say, 'You are making up things and making false allegations. It will be great if we can settle this matter mutually, otherwise it can be a prolonged legal hassle to both of us.' Keep your tone firm and assertive, but not loud or disrespectful.

If the other person is adamant and does not cooperate, leave the place after taking a picture of the accident scene, the number plate of the bike, the person's name, address and contact number, or whatever information you can gather.

Parenting by example is the best way of parenting. Keep exhibiting to your children that even crisis situations can be tackled with composure and respect.

Family Reflection Time

Discuss with your family and document your reflections about the Tadaka episode. What would you have done in Rama's place? You may want to jot down your reflections,

click a picture and share on social media with the hashtag .
#MyRamayana.

_____

_____

_____

_____

_____

Family Breakfast Discussion

Have you ever faced a situation where you faced a moral
dilemma even while seemingly doing the right thing? All
the family members can share their own cases. You may
want to jot down your reflections, click a picture and share
on social media with the hashtag **#MyRamayana**.

_____

_____

_____

_____

_____

4

Learn from the Rama vs Maricha Fight, Don't Procrastinate

After killing the demoness Tadaka, Rama and Laxmana continued their journey in the forest with Sage Vishwamitra. The sage took both the princes to his hermitage in the Dandaka forest, where he and his fellow sages performed yagnas, and where the evil demons often disturbed them. Sage Vishwamitra and his fellow sages decided to perform a Vedic* ritual for six days and six nights continuously, for the peace and prosperity of the world. And this yagna was done in the presence and protection of Rama and Laxmana.

The yagna started with the chanting of the powerful Vedic mantras. It proceeded well and went on harmoniously for the first five days. Towards its conclusion, on the last day, a frightening noise suddenly thundered in the sky.

___

* Vedic means something from the ancient Indian texts called the Vedas.

Two demons, Maricha and Subahu, the sons of demoness Tadaka, came along with their big army of demons to spoil the yagna. They attempted to throw animal flesh and blood into the sacred fire. Rama and Laxmana were fully alert to safeguard the sages and the Vedic rituals.

The princes used all the archery and warcraft skills they had learnt from their gurus Vasishtha and Vishwamitra. After a vigorous fight, they were successful in safeguarding the sages and the rituals. In Rama and Laxmana's attack, Subahu and other demons got killed. But the arrow aimed at Maricha was not strong enough. Though he was thrown away many miles into the sea, he was not killed. The problem called Maricha was put off but not solved. Later in the story, we will read how Maricha came once again into Rama's life with more trouble and played a notorious role in the abduction of Mata Sita.

Once Rama and Laxmana had dealt with all the demons, Sage Vishwamitra blessed them and took them to

Mithila, where King Janaka was organizing a Swayamvar[*] for his daughter Sita. There was a competition set for this  Swayamvar. Sita would marry only that person who would be able to string Pinaka, the mighty bow of the god Shiva. Janaka knew that ordinary mortals couldn't even lift the bow of Shiva, let alone string it. Hence, through this challenge, Janaka tried to find the best match for his daughter Sita. Many kings and princes came and failed at the task. Many were not even able to lift the bow, as expected. A few who could lift it were unable to string it. Then came Rama's turn. He lifted the bow of Shiva with his left hand, and he fastened the string and broke the bow in the process.

Rama fulfilled the condition of the Swayamvar to marry Sita. She, too, liked Rama's calm and firm personality. Parents, gurus, relatives and friends of Rama were invited to Mithila for the grand wedding ceremony. As

---

[*] Swayamvar is a process of self-selection of the groom by the girl, based on some condition or some competition of skill or intelligence.

a lovely coincidence, Rama's brothers married Sita's sisters in the same ceremony: Bharata married Mandavi, Laxmana married Urmila, and Shatrughna married Shrutakirti.

All the four princes returned to Ayodhya with their life partners. When they all returned to Ayodhya Queen Kaikeyi gifted the grand Kanaka Palace to Rama and Sita as their wedding gift.

This concludes the first part of the Ramayana, the Bala Kanda.

Life Lesson #4 for Families

Rama's arrow launched at Maricha did not kill him. Maricha was just thrown away miles into the sea. Maricha would return once again, playing a key role in the abduction of Sita. This incident teaches us that:

Problems not tackled effectively *now* will haunt
you later. So *avoid* procrastination.

Family Scenario #4

Your son Rahul is in elementary grade. One day, you notice
colour pencils, erasers, kids' watches and other fancy items
in his backpack—things that do not belong to your child.
How would you respond to this behaviour?

A) Will observe him for a couple of months, before
   intervening; he may drop the habit himself
B) Will scold and beat him up, as the child is developing
   the dangerous habit of stealing
C) Report to his teacher to keep a constant check on him
   in the future
D) Allow more freedom to him when it comes to choosing
   toys and stationery to be purchased for him

Guidance for Families from the Ramayana #4

Parents who use their children's mistakes as an opportunity
at the very early stage to instil a value in them can be assured
of avoiding bigger problems that may occur in the future.
Delaying the uncomfortable discussion with your child will
only make their bad habits grow. Eliminate the problem
called Maricha as soon as possible. Upon noticing any
mistake made by your child, the most important thing is to

approach it in a non-intimidating way. Open a conversation with an understanding attitude. Don't shame them in front of their teachers and friends. Allow the child to work upon amending the mistake, with your help if required. In many situations, the habit of stealing among children is directly correlated with the lack of opportunity given to them in terms of making decisions or choices when it comes to their parents buying things for them. So you might want to consider allowing more freedom to Rahul in this regard.

Family Reflection Time

Share with your family the past incidents where procrastination cost you heavily. You may want to jot down your reflections, click a picture and share on social media with the hashtag **#MyRamayana**.

_____

_____

_____

_____

_____

_____

_____

_____

Your Favourite Character from the Bala Kanda

Looking at the Bala Kanda, we have learnt about various characters of the Ramayana. First, list all the characters from the Bala Kanda. Then, thoughtfully choose the character you find most inspiring. Also, share why and how that character inspires you. Different family members may have different favourite characters. You may want to put down your thoughts about your favourite character, click a photo and share on social media with the hashtag **#MyRamayana**.

_____

_____

_____

_____

_____

_____

_____

_____

Kill the Ravana within You

You will agree with me that we all have both Rama- and Ravana-like qualities within us. Our first aim should be to meticulously and impartially identify our

'Rama' and 'Ravana' qualities. Then, we should work to further strengthen our Rama qualities and get rid of our Ravana qualities.

Having learnt the four important lessons from the Bala Kanda, you have already started acquiring the initial wisdom of the Ramayana. At this point in the book, which Ravana quality within you do you want to eliminate? You may want to note down your answer, click a photo and share on social media with the hashtag **#MyRamayana**.

_____

_____

_____

_____

_____

_____

_____

_____

_____

Bala Kanda Crossword Puzzle

Across

2 The very short-tempered brother of Rama

5 The golden deer

9 Janaka was the king of _____

10 Rama's wife

11 Maryada Purushottam

13 Bharata's mother

15 Kaikeyi's son

17 Maricha's brother

18 Who brought the River Ganga to the earth?

21 Priest who took Rama and Laxmana to kill rakshasas

22 Who performed Putr Kamesthi Yagna

23 The angry avatar of Maha Vishnu

Down

1 Author of the original Ramayana

3 Rama's mother

4 The youngest of the four brothers

6 Laxmana and Shatrughna's mother

7 Mother of Maricha and Subahu

8 Laxmana's wife

12 Bharata's wife

14 The royal priest of Dashratha's kingdom

16 Shatrughna's wife

19 Where was the palace of Kosala?

20 Sita's father

Find the answers on page 173

PART II

Ayodhya Kanda
Beware of Negative Company

5

Learn How to 'Walk the Talk' from King Dasharatha

By now, all the four princes were married and well trained in various aspects of statecraft. At that point, King Dasharatha was keen to choose his successor, as he was growing old. He had consultations with his court men, kings of neighbouring kingdoms and people's representatives, and Rama's name unanimously emerged as the one who was most suitable for the job.

The whole of Ayodhya was joyous on the courts' decision to coronate Rama as their next king. A day before Rama's coronation, Queen Kaikeyi, like everyone else in Ayodhya, was feeling very elated. But there was one person in the whole of Ayodhya who was not happy with Rama's upcoming coronation: it was  Kaikeyi's help Manthara. Manthara told Kaikeyi that King Dasharatha would soon die and that the new king, Rama, and his mother, Kausalya, would treat her like a maid, that she would be treated as a second-grade citizen of Ayodhya. Initially, Kaikeyi did not pay heed to Manthara's vicious constructs. But Manthara kept on poisoning Kaikeyi's mind and was finally able to convince her to ask Dasharatha to coronate Bharata as the king of Ayodhya and send Rama for fourteen years of exile.

Kaikeyi, under the influence of Manthara, decided to use the two boons King Dasharatha had given her a couple of years earlier. She asked for the crown of Ayodhya for her son Bharata and fourteen years of exile for Rama. Dasharatha went into a shock after hearing this. On the one hand, he had his two promises to keep, but, on the other hand, if he did so he would lose his son and Ayodhya would lose an able king like Rama, for fourteen long years.

Dasharatha was cognizant of the fact that no one other than he and Kaikeyi knew about the two boons. He knew that if he went back on his promise to Kaikeyi, nobody would question him—nobody but his own conscience. His dynasty was studded with kings who lived by their promises. For kings of the Ikshvaku dynasty, a promise was more valuable than anything else. King Dasharatha knew that if he did not honour his promise, the legend of keeping promises would dilute among the people of his kingdom. Finally, King Dasharatha followed the grit and tradition of his dynasty and declared: a promise is a promise and had to be kept in all circumstances. With a very heavy heart, he agreed to Kaikeyi's demands.

Though the exile was only for Rama, his wife, Sita, and brother Laxmana accompanied him, leaving all the luxuries of the palatial life. After his beloved son Rama left, King Dasharatha was heartbroken and miserable; he was unable to breathe, eat or sleep. And within a few months he died but did not allow the stain of a broken promise on his dynasty.

Life Lesson #5 for Families

There was no written agreement between King Dasharatha and Kaikeyi. And other than both of them, nobody knew about the two boons. Even then, King Dasharatha agreed to Kaikeyi's unreasonable demands, just because he had made a promise. King Dasharatha has taught humanity that one must:

> **Walk the talk.**

Family Scenario #5

Your child approached you while you were very busy with your work. He asked you to play the game of Monopoly with him. You said you will play later. The child got louder with his demand. You again explained that you would play with him in the evening. The child left with a heavy heart. What would you do in the evening?

A) Wait until the child reminds you again of Monopoly, and ignore otherwise
B) Ensure to **walk the talk** and initiate the game of Monopoly, even if the child has forgotten about it

Guidance for Families from the Ramayana #5

If you try to ignore the demands of children, they will come back louder, in their own way. If it's not the right time for something and you are genuinely busy, you can gently postpone it to another time by assuring your child that you will attend to them later.

But it is very important to build trust with your children right from childhood, by ensuring to walk your talk every single time. If your child experiences mistrust with you in your dealings, please note that you are setting the stage of non-cooperation from your child for life. So, even if the child has forgotten about it, you should initiate the game of Monopoly later in the day, when you get time. When Dasharatha can follow through on such an uncomfortable and painful promise, for the sake of keeping the promise, a game of Monopoly with your children is nothing, and it can be a fun reward in itself for keeping the promise.

Parents are the foremost role models for their children. Not being able to model the 'walk-the-talk' principle in real-life situations can give the signal to the child that keeping a promise is not always necessary.

Family Reflection Time

Discuss with your family and document your reflections about the Kaikeyi incident, which changed the course of Rama's life. You may want to jot down your reflections,

click a picture and share on social media with the hashtag
#MyRamayana.

_____

_____

_____

_____

_____

_____

Family Breakfast Discussion

As a family, do you think that Kaikeyi was instrumental in
the elimination of Ravana, since Rama went to the jungle
because of her boons? You may want to note down your
thoughts, click a picture and share on social media with the
hashtag **#MyRamayana**.

_____

_____

_____

_____

_____

_____

6

Beware of Bad Counsel: When Kaikeyi Received Manthara's Wrong Advice

Kaikeyi loved Rama like her own son. In fact, Kaikeyi was so fond of Rama that she gifted the grand Kanaka Palace to Rama and Sita after their return from Mithila kingdom. Kaikeyi was the happiest when Rama's name was chosen by Dasharatha's court after intense deliberations. But Manthara's parochial and selfish advice corrupted Kaikeyi. Though it took time for Manthara to brainwash Kaikeyi, eventually she succeeded to poison the queen's mind.

From the day Rama left for exile, Kaikeyi was disliked by every single citizen of Ayodhya. Her husband, Dasharatha, died of the grief that was caused by Kaikeyi's actions. Bharata, her own son, for whom Kaikeyi had plotted the whole coup, detested her for her heinous act. Bharata disliked Kaikeyi's machinations so much that he said he was ashamed to have been born to Kaikeyi. Bharata never wanted that throne, and he never sat on it. Kaikeyi's plot went in vain, and she became synonymous with 'bad mother' in history because of Manthara's ill-intentioned advice.

Some scholars give the credit for Ravana's demise to Kaikeyi. They argue that Rama went to exile because of Kaikeyi's boons, which created the opportunity for Rama and Ravana's battle and for the eventual elimination of the dreaded demon Ravana. I sincerely believe that this logic is flawed. Kaikeyi and Manthara did not execute their plot for any higher purpose for humanity. Kaikeyi was blinded by Manthara's ill-intentioned advice and executed her plans. Rama had taken birth as the seventh avatar of Vishnu to eliminate negativity, to eliminate asuras and to eliminate Ravana. So Rama would have created the opportunity to kill Ravana anyhow, even without Kaikeyi's plot.

Life Lesson #6 for Families

Kaikeyi was fundamentally a good-natured woman but was convinced to send Rama into exile and insisted that her son Bharata be crowned as the king by Manthara, whom she considered loyal and wise. On the other hand, Manthara's bad counsel not only poisoned Kaikeyi's mind into demanding those two appalling boons but also ruined her reputation. This incident teaches us that we should:

Beware of bad counsel.

Family Scenario #6

Auro and Pushkar were best friends in school. They would compete with each other healthily in academics and sports, but would also support each other in preparations. Pushkar stood first in the closely contested annual maths Olympiad. Auro came second. Both Pushkar and Auro treated each other for their respective achievements. Rahul was jealous of Pushkar and Auro's close friendship. He used this as an opportunity and poisoned Auro's mind against Pushkar. Rahul made Auro believe that Pushkar had used him for Olympiad preparations but did not share his own notes with Auro. Rahul succeeded in creating a rift between Auro and Puskar, and it started affecting their performance in sports and academics. As a counsellor in school, how will you advise Auro and Pushkar?

A) Life has many competitions. You win some and lose some. So don't take your losses to heart.
B) Bad advice is like a slow poison. Do filter such advice thoroughly.
C) Friends come and go. Focus on your personal growth and move on.

Guidance for Families from the Ramayana #6

Good friends are very valuable in life. One should not lose them for frivolous reasons. The story of Manthara's bad advice to Kaikeyi is a perfect one to narrate to Auro: How Manthara's vicious scheming poisoned Kaikeyi's mind and how, as a result, she lost her beloved husband's life, lost the love and respect of her son Bharata, and earned herself the title of 'bad mother' for life.

This is a very important lesson for your children, about how to differentiate between good and bad advice. It teaches them to stay on guard against vicious counsel. It teaches them to be vigilant. It teaches them to have a firm mind and not get swayed easily.

Family Reflection Time

Discuss with your family and document your reflections on how Kaikeyi was corrupted by Manthara's vicious thoughts. You may want note down your reflections, click a picture and share on social media with the hashtag **#MyRamayana**.

_____

_____

_____

_____

_____

_____

_____

_____

_____

Idioms and Phrases from the Ramayana

Construct a sentence using the phrase 'Manthara advice' instead of 'bad advice'.

For example: When Rahul tried to poison Auro's mind against Pushkar, Auro stopped him and said, 'Don't give me the Manthara advice.'

_____

_____

_____

_____

_____

_____

_____

_____

_____

_____

7

Negative Company Can Bring You Bad Reputation: Learn from Bharata

After a few days, Bharata and Shatrughna returned to Ayodhya. To their shock and dismay, it was not the same Ayodhya that they had left. Their father was dead, their beloved brothers, Rama and Laxmana, and sister-in-law Mata Sita were in exile, and the people of Ayodhya were in a constant state of mourning.

Bharata was outraged by his mother Kaikeyi and Manthara's plot. Kaikeyi tried to calm him and entice him with the kingship of Ayodhya. But Bharata was very clear: Rama was chosen as the next king, and so Rama deserved to be on the throne, not Bharata. He announced that he would be going to search for Rama and would bring him back at any cost.

Bharata set out to find Rama in the jungle. He was determined that he would be able to convince Rama to return. He was sure that Rama would oblige his beloved younger brother. The common people of Ayodhya, people from the courtroom of Ayodhya, soldiers, the three mothers and all the saints and advisers in the court—everyone joined Bharata in his search for Rama. They all wanted to have a glimpse of Rama. They all wanted him back in Ayodhya.

Nishadraj Guha and Rishi Bhardwaj helped them to navigate through the jungle and gave clues on how to trace Rama. When the whole team was about to reach Chitrakoot, where Rama was living, Laxmana heard the uproar. He climbed on a tree and was surprised to see so many people approaching them under Bharata's leadership. He went and informed Rama and Sita that Bharata was coming to kill Rama, so that he could rule without any interruption even after fourteen years of exile. In fact, initially, Nishadraj Guha and Rishi Bhardwaj had also thought the same about Bharata. Everyone had thought that Bharata had teamed up with Kaikeyi and Manthara in their vicious plot.

As it happened with Bharata, even slight proximity with negative company can bring bad reputation to anyone.

Life Lesson #7 for Families

Bharata was going to search and convince his brother Rama to come back to Ayodhya and take on the throne, which only Rama deserved. But Guha, Rishi Bhardwaj and even Laxmana thought that Bharata was going to kill Rama—they all thought that Bharata had teamed up with Kaikeyi and Manthara in their vicious plans. This situation teaches us that:

> **Bad company and associations give you a bad reputation.**

Family Scenario #7

You shifted to a new city, Pune, because of your new job. Your son was not so happy with this move, as he had to leave his society friends and school friends in Delhi. Initial months were a little tough for him. Then he started making friends. But his behaviour has become a little different from his days in Delhi. He now spends long hours on online gaming, uses foul words often and lies frequently. One day, his class teacher calls you and warns you that your child seems to have fallen into bad company. He quickly picks up fights, has started using abusive words and is not focused in the class. The teacher adds that he seems to have picked up some not-so-good friends, in his colony as well as in school. What will be your reaction in such a situation?

A) You will call your son in front of the teacher and shout at your son, asking him about his newly acquired bad company of friends

B) You will try to follow his routine more closely for the next 2–3 weeks and find out who his friends are

C) You will sit with your son and tell him how important it is to be with friends who can help us grow and improve us as a person

Guidance for Families from the Ramayana #7

Though your son is very smart and intelligent, he is in his teens. So he may not be able to make the best choices and decisions for himself all the time. You understand how the teenage period is—full of emotions and mood swings that need special care, attention and understanding. Making mistakes is a huge part of growing up, and giving children space to learn through their mistakes is important for parents. Spend time with your children, have conversations, ask about their day, tell them about your day as a usual dinner conversation. It is very important to keep a subtle, non-intrusive eye on where and with whom your child is spending time. Instead of scolding them, use this as an opportunity to get closer to your child and help them develop a sense of good judgement. Tell them, with examples from your own childhood, how good and bad company positively and negatively affected your life. Narrating Bharata's incident from the Ramayana will surely add value to the discussion with your child. When your teenager makes a mistake, consider that you, too, have made a parenting mistake, and you both have to correct these mistakes.

Family Reflection Time

Discuss with your family and document your reflections on how Bharata earned a bad reputation through his perceived connivance with Kaikeyi and Manthara. You may want to note down your reflections, click a picture and share on social media with the hashtag #MyRamayana.

_____

_____

_____

_____

_____

_____

_____

_____

_____

Family Breakfast Discussion

How do you think Bharata should have managed the wrong perception about his alliance with the conspirators against Rama? You may want to note down your thoughts, click a picture and share on social media with the hashtag **#MyRamayana**.

_____

_____

_____

_____

_____

_____

_____

8

Learn from Bharata: Never Appropriate Anything That Is Not Rightfully Yours

Guha, Rishi Bhardwaj and Laxmana thought that Bharata was coming to Chitrakoot to eliminate Rama. But Rama himself was calm and told Laxmana to let Bharata come. Rama had full trust in Bharata. Bharata's mind was filled with multiple contradictory emotions when he met his beloved brother Rama. He was embarrassed because of his mother Kaikeyi's ploy to dethrone Rama. He was sad about their father's death. He was pained because of Ayodhya's miserable condition after Rama's exile. He was determined to bring Rama back, to set things right.

Bharata pleaded with the utmost humility, love and respect to Rama, and asked him to return to Ayodhya and rule it as a king. All three mothers, all the sages, people from the court and citizens requested Rama to return in their own earnest way. But Rama refused. Rama said that he was bound by the promise he had given to his father,

to be in exile for fourteen years. For his part, Bharata too declared that he would not go back to Ayodhya till Rama agreed to return. Rama was in no mood to breach the promise he had made to his father. Both the brothers were determined on their positions. It was a deadlock. Both were right, both wanted the best for each other and their beloved kingdom, Ayodhya.

Observing the deadlock, Rishi Vasishtha intervened and suggested that Bharata become the proxy, or representative, of King Rama for the next fourteen years, till Rama completes his exile and returns to Ayodhya. This idea was agreeable to both Rama and Bharata. Rama did not want to break the promise he had made to his father, and Bharata did not want to take up the kingship, which was not rightfully his. Rishi Vasishtha, and everyone present there, was overwhelmed by this divine contest of virtues between the two brothers.

Bharata accepted Rishi Vasishtha's advice but just kept one condition: that he would take Rama's slippers, or the *charan padukas*, and place them on the throne of Ayodhya. Rama graciously agreed to his brother's request.

For fourteen long years Bharata ruled Ayodhya as the representative of Rama. Bharata left all the royal amenities and the palace. He made a hut in a nearby village called Nandigram, where he lived for those fourteen years. From there he ruled as Rama's representative with the help of his brother Shatrughna. He left all the princely privileges and decided to live an almost exiled life, like that of Rama, Sita and Laxmana in the jungle.

Life Lesson #8 for Families

Bharata could have easily ruled Ayodhya as a king for fourteen years. There was no one to question him. King Dasharatha was dead, and Rama and Laxmana were away from Ayodhya. It was too lucrative an offer to refuse. But Bharata knew that Rama had been chosen as the king and was more suitable for the position. Bharata's sacrifice teaches us that we should:

> **Never appropriate anything that is not rightfully ours.**

Family Scenario #8

Your child's school is sending two students for a regional-level archery competition. The school has shortlisted two students based on skill level and competence. As your child missed the selection and was disappointed, you decided to use some influence through his private coach to facilitate your child's entry in the competition. As a result, one of the previously selected students was replaced by your child. What would be your take in such situation?

A) You would be happy and proud that your child got the opportunity to participate in a regional-level competition
B) You would re-evaluate your decision and withdraw your child from the competition for the greater benefit of the school
C) You would provide more and better training to your child so that he gets selected the next time, based on merit

Guidance for Families from the Ramayana #8

In families, adults often tend to focus on achieving things, goals and desires by using shortcuts that are not always based on fair means. In such a pursuit of reaching the desired end result, the process and means of attaining the result are ignored conveniently.

It is important to understand, in order to set an example for others in the family, that when the act of achieving our goals is based on integrity, genuine efforts and the consideration of others, it builds your character, and you get long-term rewards.

Bharata was unambiguously sure that he would not appropriate the kingship of Ayodhya, which was not rightfully his. When the fundamental principle of not appropriating anything which one is not entitled to is followed at the family level, the corruption at a larger, societal level can be rooted out, resulting in a progressive, non-corrupt society.

Family Reflection Time

Discuss with your family and document your reflections on Bharata's supreme sacrifice. You may want to jot down your reflections, click a picture and share on social media with the hashtag #MyRamayana.

_____

_____

_____

_____

_____

_____

Family Breakfast Discussion

Do you think Bharata's ultimate sacrifice gets unnoticed in
the popular narration of the Ramayana? You may want to
jot down your thoughts, click a picture and share on social
media with the hashtag **#MyRamayana**.

_____

_____

_____

_____

_____

_____

_____

_____

9

When You Get Lemons, Make Lemonade: Nobody Lived up to This Better Than Rama

During their exile, Rama, Laxmana and Sita had taken a vow to survive on fruits, roots and water (*fala, moola, jala*). By the time Bharata came to meet Rama at Chitrakoot, the exiled trio had struggled enough and found the basic means of survival at Chitrakoot. Chitrakoot is in today's Uttar Pradesh. But after Bharata's visit, that hideout became known to many in Ayodhya. Rama knew that many people from Ayodhya would start visiting him frequently at Chitrakoot, which would make him weak, and he might develop a longing to go back to Ayodhya. So he decided to leave Chitrakoot and move further into the deadly jungle of Dandkaranya along with Sita and Laxman.

For almost the next twelve years, Rama did not set up a proper base and kept on moving from one guru to another. His quest for knowledge and wisdom took him to hermits like Rishi Bhardwaja, Rishi Valmiki, Rishi Atri, Rishi

Sharabhanga, Rishi Agastya and many more. He learnt new dimensions of spirituality, philosophy, statecraft, warcraft and justice.

This was the same Rama who had lost his kingdom just a day before his coronation. Someone who had been brought up in the luxuries of the palace was now fending for food, shelter and safety for himself, his wife and his brother every day. But he never complained about his ill fate, never said that he wanted those fourteen tough years to be over soon so that he could be back to his smooth palatial life. On the contrary, he made the best of every day of his exile. He searched for the best of gurus and learnt rare skills. He upgraded himself as a human being.

The knowledge and wisdom he acquired during those years helped him to contain and calm himself during the later challenges of exile, and enabled him to emerge victorious.

And that concludes the Ayodhya Kanda.

Life Lesson #9 for Families

Rama was getting ready to be anointed as the king of Ayodhya when he heard the decision that he was being exiled for fourteen years. Instead of crying over his fate, Rama made the best use of those years in exile to become a better person. He started his exile as Prince Rama or King Rama, and by virtue of his constant learnings and the character he developed during exile, he returned as Lord Rama. Rama teaches us:

> **When you get lemons, make lemonade.**

Family Scenario #9

After returning from the USA, Mohan made a beautiful house in Mumbai. The whole family soon got used to the Indian way of life and started enjoying their new home. The house was in a low-lying area. So during one of the floods in the city, it got deluged. This caused a lot of damage to the furniture, expensive artworks and books, and derailed their daily life. Different family members reacted differently to this. Think about what your reaction would be to such an episode.

A) You will obviously feel very perturbed with the damage and loss and would be unable to think how to handle it
B) You will take the whole family to an alternative location and wait for the flood to recede
C) You will try to stay strong and constantly evaluate the situation; you will motivate each member of the family to contribute ideas to arrive at the best solution for the given situation; you will use this loss to bring the family together, make them a more cohesive unit and work to their strengths

Guidance for Families from the Ramayana #9

Time does not remain constant for any of us. There are good phases and bad ones. We all obviously cherish our good times, but challenging situations help us immensely to grow as humans. In a parent's role, it becomes essential for us to teach our children to regard challenges as opportunities to grow rather than crib about them. Like Rama, we should think of challenges as classrooms where we learn life skills.

In fact, adverse phases of life make us stretch our limits and help us realize our true potential. People with such an attitude are open to new experiences and cherish challenges, so that they can learn more about themselves during such phases.

Family Reflection Time

Share with your family and friends how you made good use of your time during the Covid lockdown. You may want to note down your reflections, click a picture and share on social media with the hashtag **#MyRamayana**.

_____

_____

_____

_____

_____

_____

_____

_____

_____

Your Favourite Character from the Ayodhya Kanda

In the Ayodhya Kanda we have learnt about various characters of the Ramayana. First, list all the characters from the Ayodhya Kanda. Then, thoughtfully choose the character whom you find most inspiring. Also, share why and how that character inspires you. Different family members may have different favourite characters. You may want jot down your thoughts about your favourite character, click a picture and share on social media with the hashtag #MyRamayana.

_____

_____

_____

_____

_____

_____

_____

_____

_____

_____

Kill the Ravana within You

As we reach the end of the Ayodhya Kanda, let's take a moment to identify our 'Rama' and 'Ravana' qualities again. We should work to further strengthen our Rama qualities and get rid of our Ravana qualities. Having learnt the five important lessons from the Ayodhya Kanda, you are moving steadily to master the essence of the Ramayana. At this point in the book, which Ravanas within you do you want to eliminate? You may want note down your answer, click a picture and share on social media with the hashtag **#MyRamayana**.

_____

_____

_____

_____

_____

_____

_____

_____

_____

_____

Ayodhya Kanda Crossword Puzzle

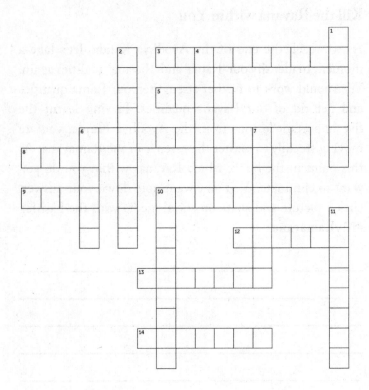

Across

3 _____ killed Shravan Kumar unintentionally

5 Kaikeyi asked Dasharatha to send _____ to exile

6 Shantanu and Gyanvanti's son

8 _____ took Rama, Sita and Laxmana in his boat

9 _____ followed her husband to the forest

10 Kaikeyi was blinded by _____'s love

12 Bharata returned with Rama's _____ to Ayodhya

13 _____ also went with Rama and Sita to the forest

14 Tadaka was in the forest of _____

Down

1 Her two boons changed the story of Ramayana

2 Where did Rama–Bharata milap happen?

4 _____ went to drop Rama, Sita and Laxmana to forest

6 Rama, Sita and Laxmana crossed _____with Guha

7 _____ poisoned Kaikeyi's mind

10 _____ advised Rama to go to Chitrakoot

11 The first wife of Dasharatha

Find the answers on page 173

PART III

Aranya[*] Kanda
Bad Choices Lead to Bad Outcomes

---

[*] Aranya means jungle.

10

Every Action Should Be Calculated: Learn This from Laxmana

After moving from one guru's ashram to another in search of knowledge and wisdom in the furious jungle of Dandakaranya for almost twelve years, Rama was advised by Rishi Agastya to spend the remaining time of his exile in Panchavati. (Panchavati is in today's Maharashtra, near Nasik.) Rama moved to Panchavati after a long journey through Dandakaranya and gradually settled there with Sita and Laxmana.

One day, a demoness named Surpanakha was passing from there, and noticed Rama and Laxmana. She was charmed by Rama's personality and approached him in the disguise of a beautiful lady. She asked him to marry her. Rama outrightly refused her offer and said that he was already married and had taken the 'one-life, one-wife vow' (*eka patni vrata*).

After Rama's refusal, she approached Laxmana with the same offer. Laxmana, too, refused to marry her. She was disappointed, humiliated and angry. She then noticed Sita there and presumed her to be the reason for Rama's refusal. In her outrage, Surpanakha ferociously attempted to attack Sita.

Ensuring Rama and Sita's safety and well-being was the single goal of Laxmana's life. He was unable to tolerate the sight of Sita being  attacked; he treated her as his mother. In a sudden rage, Laxmana cut Surpanakha's nose and ears. This single act of Laxmana became the biggest reason for the conflict between Rama and Ravana, though one may argue that the conflict between Rama and Ravana was ultimately useful for humanity.

Life Lesson #10 for Families

Laxmana was a leader in his own capacity. A leader's actions have wider repercussions. His intention to defend Mata Sita was perfect. But he could have achieved the same by firmly asking Surpanakha to stop and sending her away with a strong warning. This incident teaches us that:

> **Triggers for big disputes may appear trivial, and every action of a leader should be calculated.**

Family Scenario #10

Vivek and Nandini, parents of Anuj and Mrunal, are committed to the upbringing of their children. They wish to teach them good values, to provide the best education and living conditions to them. But they exhibit a significantly aggressive approach in solving any sort of conflicts between them, with relatives or with any strangers. In spite of their best efforts, the children grow up as insensitive, inflexible and impatient. What according to you might be the reasons for this?

A) The children took advantage of the love and care they were given, and grew up as spoiled kids
B) The children grew up in a confused environment, where what they heard and what they saw weren't in harmony
C) The parents failed to be mindful in calculating the effect of their aggressive approach on their children in the long term, in spite of the best intentions

Guidance for Families from the Ramayana #10

In families, parents are the first teachers and role models to their children. As leaders of the family, they have multiple responsibilities. Showering unconditional love on children, caring for children's needs, modelling behaviour and conduct mindfully to develop a value-based character in children, planning for the children's future in a pragmatic manner are among the prime responsibilities of parents.

Fulfilling these responsibilities requires conscious effort, mindfulness and stability of the mind and character in parents. To enable such a state of mind, there should be harmony between one's thoughts, words and actions. As a parent and leader of the family, you need to exhibit a stable mind; your actions should not be controlled by your emotions. Decisions taken under the impact of impulsive emotions tend to generally obscure the sight of possible consequences, as happened with Laxmana.

Family Reflection Time

Discuss with your family and document your reflections on how else Laxmana could have countered Surpanakha, instead of cutting her nose and ears. You may want to jot down your thoughts, click a picture and share on social media with the hashtag **#MyRamayana**.

_____

_____

_____

_____

_____

_____

_____

_____

_____

Family Breakfast Discussion

Discuss other incidents from history where any leader's trivial action might have resulted in a big battle? You may want to note down your thoughts, click a picture and share on social media with the hashtag **#MyRamayana**.

_____

_____

_____

_____

_____

_____

_____

_____

11

Everything That Glitters Is Not Gold: The Elusive Golden Deer Proves This

Surpanakha did not take this insult by Laxmana casually. She went to Khar and Dushan, Ravana's henchmen in the Panchavati area of Dandakaranya. In response, Khar and Dushan attacked Rama and Laxmana with a powerful and large army. Rama and Laxmana had convincingly defeated Khar and Dushan by using all the skills of warcraft they had learnt from their gurus. But now the word had travelled to the mighty Ravana.

A couple of days after this incident, on a bright sunny day, Sita saw an illustrious golden deer in front of their hut. She felt extremely attracted to it and asked Rama to get that deer for her to play with. Laxmana warned Mata Sita against it. He said that since they had messed with Surpanakha, Khar and Dushan recently, the opponents may strike back with some illusive trick. But Sita was adamant. The dazzling golden deer had occupied her attention. Rama followed his beloved wife's wish and asked Laxman to guard Sita. He ventured out into the jungle, chasing the golden deer.

The golden deer was fast and agile. It took Rama deep into the jungle. After a while, Rama realized that the deer could disappear and reappear. Rama started getting the sense that Laxmana was right—this golden deer seemed to be more than just a deer. But now Rama had taken up the challenge. He was the best archer of his time. He could shoot just by listening to the sound of the target with his *shabda-bhedi* (sound-guided) arrows. The deer's hide and seek game did not last long. Rama's arrow pierced the deer. As the arrow hit the deer, it turned into his original form: the demon Maricha.

The glittery, shiny and illustrious golden deer, in reality, was neither golden nor a deer. It was the elusive and malicious Maricha impersonating a golden deer. The problem called Maricha, which Rama had left unsolved in his teens, had come back to cause trouble to him and his family.

Life Lesson #11 for Families

Sita got attracted by the glitter and shine of the golden deer. But in reality, the glittery, shiny and illustrious golden deer was neither 'golden' nor a 'deer'. In life, we are often attracted by the outer appearance of things and people. On this basis, we make our decisions and regret them later. This incident teaches us that:

> **Everything that glitters is not gold.**

Family Scenario #11

Monish is in the eleventh grade. He has been growing up in a middle-class family. He is an intelligent and good-looking boy. Since he got his own mobile phone, his desire for branded things, gadgets and high fashion has increased immensely. To fulfil this desire, he has secretly started doing odd jobs to earn extra money, without telling his parents. What do you think can be the reasons Monish adopted the wrong means?

A) With the new mobile phone, Monish got on to social media platforms, where he witnessed his peers and their families using branded things, which may have attracted him

B) Monish attends birthday parties of his school friends and wants to imitate their fashion sense and lifestyle

C) Monish's parents have a simple lifestyle, so he is getting attracted to a flamboyant lifestyle

Guidance for Families from the Ramayana #11

Not only children but adults, too, get attracted to the outer appearance of people and things. We marry partners who look good; we make friends based on their appearance; the primary factor influencing us to buy things is also based on appearances. Social media amplifies such behaviour multifold. On social media platforms, we constantly see pictures of our friends partying, holidaying, travelling, shopping, etc. It augments our sense of comparison, and it's very natural for us to long for those things. This behaviour also manifests in children. In such situations, we, as parents, have to lead by example. We have to rationally explain the fine difference between need and want. We have to compensate a child's longing for expensive brands and items with some high-quality experiences, like going for trekking, camping, book shows, guided walks, etc., with the whole family. Instead of denouncing social media use, we should encourage our children to follow good handles, blogs and podcasts, so that they consume wisdom with fun. The episode featuring the golden deer and Mata Sita is a perfect example to explain to children the idea that appearances can be deceptive.

Family Reflection Time

Discuss with your family and share incidents when you got swayed by the glitter of something and faced negative consequences. You may want to note down your reflections, click a picture and share on social media with the hashtag **#MyRamayana**.

_____

_____

_____

_____

_____

_____

Idioms and Phrases from the Ramayana

Construct a sentence using the phrase 'Golden-Deerish'.

Example: Tara's mother told her that in the delicious-looking, Golden-Deerish pastry, the Maricha of bad health is hidden.

_____

_____

_____

_____

_____

_____

12

Flouting Rules Can Endanger Your Life: Learn This from Mother Sita's Folly

The glittery, shiny and illustrious golden deer, in reality, was Maricha impersonating a golden deer. True to his master Ravana, even while dying, Maricha played one more trick: he mimicked Rama's voice and shouted, 'Save me Sita! Save me Laxmana!'

Hearing Rama's outcry for help, Sita got restless and asked Laxmana to rush for Rama's help. Laxmana had sensed this as a vicious trick of Maricha. But on Sita's constant persuasion, he had to go. Rama had given him the task to protect Sita in all circumstances. Before leaving for the woods to help Rama, Laxmana, by virtue of his spiritual powers, drew a protective Laxmana Rekha* around the hut and advised Mata Sita to not cross it at any cost.

Ravana was watching his plot getting executed, hiding behind the bushes. As soon as Laxmana left, Ravana came

---

* Rekha means a line.

in the form of a saint and asked for food in front of the hut. Serving a saint is the biggest virtue on earth—Sita was brought up with such ethos. She arranged whatever was available to eat at that moment in a basket and requested the saint to come near the hut to accept the food. But the saint was adamant that he be served where he was standing. Sita was in two minds whether to follow Laxmana's instruction of not crossing the Laxmana Rekha or the saint's request to serve him crossing the Laxmana Rekha.

She wanted blessings for her family from the saint and overlooked Laxmana's warning to not cross the line. As soon she was in the proximity of the saint, Ravana turned into his real self and, grabbing Mata Sita by her wrist, took her away towards the south in his famous aerial chariot, Pushpaka Vimana.*

Ravana's plot of kidnapping Sita worked as per his evil desires.

And that concludes the Aranya Kanda.

---

* Vimana refers to a flying chariot.

Life Lesson #12 for Families

Laxmana had set the rule of not crossing the Laxmana Rekha for Sita's safety and security. But Mother Sita got overwhelmed by the saint's persuasion and flouted the rule, and got into deep trouble. This incident teaches us that:

> **Rules are meant to be followed and flouting them
> can endanger your life.**

Family Scenario #12

Every family, community, society, city, state and country puts in place a certain set of rules and guidelines for harmonious functioning. Please reflect and select from the following options to see how you are placed as an individual, family and citizen in terms of your attitude towards rules and guidelines.

A) I largely respect rules and try to follow them as per my convenience, if there's no hassle involved in following it
B) I think most people don't follow rules, and my not following rules will not create much of a problem either
C) I adhere to the set rules and guidelines with the intention of influencing fellow human beings

Guidance for Families from the Ramayana #12

Rules are meant for one's safety and well-being. Rules and guidelines are framed by people who have expertise and wisdom, and they are meant to create an environment for harmonious living in society. For instance, during the Covid pandemic, governments across the globe set the rule of wearing masks in public and social distancing to prevent the virus from spreading. By following rules, elders in the family can set a model behaviour for the other members of the family to follow. Flouting rules may look exciting and cool for a short while, but it only adds to problems in the longer run. Some meaningful suggestions to amend the rules to make them more practical and efficient are always welcomed in any progressive society. It is good to remind ourselves that chaos and mishaps happened in the lives of Mata Sita, Rama and Laxmana when Mata Sita overlooked the rule set by Laxmana.

Family Reflection Time

Discuss with your family and share your thoughts on what you would have done in such a situation if you were in

Sita's place? You may want to jot down your reflections, click a picture and share on social media with the hashtag **#MyRamayana**.

_____

_____

_____

_____

_____

_____

Idioms and Phrases from the Ramayana

Construct a sentence using the term 'Laxmana Rekha'.

Example: The teacher asked students not to cross the thin Laxmana Rekha of the teacher–student relationship.

_____

_____

_____

_____

_____

_____

_____

Your Favourite Character from the Aranya Kanda

In the Aranya Kanda, we learnt about various characters of the Ramayana. First, list all the characters from the Aranya Kanda. Then, thoughtfully choose the character whom you find most inspiring. Also share why and how that character inspires you. Different family members may have different favourite characters. You may want to note down your thoughts about your favourite character, click a photo and share on social media with the hashtag **#MyRamayana**.

_____

_____

_____

_____

_____

_____

_____

Kill the Ravana within You

Now you have completed almost half of the Ramayana. At the end of the Aranya Kanda, let's take a moment to identify our 'Rama' and 'Ravana' qualities again. Then we should work to further strengthen our Rama qualities and get rid of our Ravana qualities. After learning the three important lessons from the Aranya Kanda, you are moving towards the war-related kandas of the Ramayana. At this point in the book, which Ravanas within you do you want to eliminate? You may want to jot down your answer, click a picture and share on social media with the hashtag **#MyRamayana**.

_____

_____

_____

_____

_____

_____

_____

Aranya Kanda Crossword Puzzle

Across

2 Ravana's cousin, a man-eating rakshasa

4 She wanted the golden deer

8 Sita was kidnapped from _____

9 Ravana took Sita towards the _____

10 Dashanan

Down

1 He ran after the golden deer

2 The headless monster

3 Laxmana cut her nose

5 _____turned into a golden deer

6 He went in search of Rama, hearing him cry in pa

7 Twin brother of Khar

Find the answers on page 173

PART IV

Kishkinda Kanda
Value of Strategic Partnership in Life

13

Strategic Partnerships Can Take You Places: Learn How Rama Made Alliances

After the golden deer fiasco, when Rama and Laxmana returned from the jungle, they did not find any trace of Sita near the hut until they met the wounded Jatayu. Jatayu, a bird, had seen the act of kidnapping by Ravana and resisted him bravely. Jatayu knew that he was no match for the mighty Ravana, but that didn't deter  him from attempting to stop Ravana. Before the profusely bleeding Jatayu fell on the ground, he shared that Ravana had taken Mata Sita towards the south through the aerial route.

Rama and Laxmana followed the direction through the position of stars. On the way they met an ardent devotee of Rama: Shabri, who had heard great things about Rama from many travelling saints and had been waiting for Rama for many years. She fed Rama some of the sweetest berries available in the jungle. She tasted each berry to check for its sweetness. Rama did not mind eating those half-eaten berries.

Further ahead, they met a weird-looking demon, Kabanda. Kabanda attempted to attack Rama and Laxmana. After a brief fight, Kabanda succumbed and guided them to collaborate with the exiled king Sugriva in the hills of Kishkinda.*

---

* Kishkinda corresponds to the Hampi region in the Bellary district of today's Karnataka.

When Rama and Laxmana reached the foothills of Kishkinda, Sugriva saw them from the top of the hill and suspected them to be the henchmen sent by his brother Bali to eliminate him. Their attire further added to Sugriva's suspicion; they were wearing clothes of a hermit but carrying bow and arrow like warriors. Sugriva sent his most trusted lieutenant, Hanuman, to check on the two young men.

Hanuman went to see Rama and Laxmana as a saint and asked who they were. Rama graciously introduced himself as Dashrath's exiled son and transparently narrated the whole incident of his wife's kidnapping and Kabanda's suggestion that they should partner with Sugriva for Sita's search. It took no time for Hanuman to assess Rama's divinity and genuineness. At the same time, Rama himself got impressed with Hanuman's communication skills. Rama told Laxmana that Hanuman's ability to communicate well showed that he must have had access to some profound teacher. Rama emphasized that Hanuman's sentence formation and his understanding of Sanskrit vocabulary and grammar were scholarly, and his enunciation extremely melodious. Rama and Hanuman connected at a different spiritual level at their very first meeting.

After he had done his due diligence, Hanuman took Rama and Laxmana to Sugriva. Rama and Sugriva narrated their life stories to each other, which had two uncanny similarities—both had been exiled from their kingdoms and both were away from their wives. Both agreed to help each other to create a strategic, win-win partnership. Rama promised Sugriva to assist him in getting his kingdom and wife, Ruma, back. Sugriva promised Rama that he would do whatever it took to search for Sita.

Life Lesson #13 for Families

Rama and Sugriva both agreed to help each other to create a strategic, win-win partnership. Rama promised Sugriva to assist him in getting his kingdom and wife back. Sugriva promised Rama that he would help him in his search for Sita. This incident teaches us that:

> **Thoughtful, win-win, strategic partnerships can take you places.**

Family Scenario #13

Ritu and Sanjay, a couple, are both very talented individuals. Ritu is an apt homemaker with great skills of home management, communication and parenting. She thoroughly enjoys her role. Sanjay is a photographer by profession and is in demand for his art, creativity and aesthetic sense. Despite the fact that they were gifted with special talents and involved in what they loved doing, there was a constant lack of contentment in their relationship. Ritu felt Sanjay didn't respect her enough for being a homemaker when she was so dedicated towards their home. Ritu often point out that Sanjay had a fun life and got to travel a lot in his profession, whereas she had to be mostly home. What do you think are the possible solutions to bring harmony and a sense of contentment in such a relationship?

A) Both of them should involve a common friend and speak their minds out

B) Each of them should fulfil their roles as best as they can

C) Sanjay can take Ritu along sometimes on his photoshoots; Ritu and Sanjay can enjoy the experience of travelling together, and Ritu can also take care of Sanjay's things with her homemaking skills

Guidance for Families from the Ramayana #13

Two people together make up a relationship, so that they complement each other and grow as human beings. The idea of a mutually rewarding companionship has to do with combining your strengths to help each other as well help yourselves, the way Rama and Sugriva did. Your life partner is a part of your body, soul and system. So if you hurt your partner, you are in a way throwing an axe on your leg. If you throw an axe on your leg, how far will you be able to run? Respect each other's strength and role in life to create a win-win proposition.

Family Reflection Time

Discuss with your family and share your reflections on Rama and Sugriva's win-win partnership. You may want to jot down your reflections, click a picture and share on social media with the hashtag #MyRamayana.

_____

_____

_____

_____

_____

Family Breakfast Discussion

Share examples with your family about the time when you created an impactful and strategic win-win partnership.

_____

_____

_____

_____

_____

_____

_____

_____

14

Realize the Power of Clear Communication: Bali and Sugriva Became Victims of Lack of Communication

Rama was curious to know how the two brothers Bali and Sugriva became enemies. When asked, Sugriva narrated the incident to Rama. Bali was the king of Kishkinda, and Sugriva was the second-in-command. Once a demon called

Dundubhi came to Kishkinda to create havoc in the city. Bali killed him and saved his city. To take revenge for Dundubhi's death, his brother Mayavi came to Kishkinda. Bali and Sugriva came out to neutralize him. It so happened that Bali and Mayavi got into a brawl and went into a cave fighting vigorously. Bali made Sugriva stand outside the cave, as back-up. Bali and Mayavi's fight went on for a long time. Then came a loud scream of pain. It sounded like Bali's voice. Sugriva thought Bali got killed inside the cave, and so he closed the opening of the cave with a big boulder, so that Mayavi couldn't come out.

But in reality, Bali had killed Mayavi inside the cave and made a loud victory cry. When Bali came towards the opening of the cave, he found it closed. He thought Sugriva did not want him to come out, planning to install himself as a king. Bali pushed the boulder, came out in a rage and banished Sugriva out of the kingdom. Bali's anger made him vicious and he also kept Sugriva's wife, Ruma, with him.

This classic form of miscommunication between Bali and Sugriva led to enormous animosity between the two brothers.

Life Lesson #14 for Families

Bali and Sugriva did not bother to investigate the situation, did not communicate clearly, made assumptions based on their biases and created a lot of confusion. This incident clearly teaches us that we should:

> **Realize the power of clear communication and never assume.**

Family Scenario #14

Santosh, Leena and their son, Raghav, live together with Raghav's grandparents in the same house as a family of five members. All members seem to have good intentions towards each other, maintaining harmony in the family. But there is an observable suffocation and distance between family members, which, in spite of their good financial and social status and good health, doesn't allow peace and joy in the family. What, according to you, may be the reasons?

A) What the family members expect of each other is not reasonable and hence never fulfilled, resulting in continued dissatisfaction
B) Members assess situations by assumptions and don't prefer to clarify their assumptions
C) Clarification as a tool to sort out misunderstandings is often seen as an offensive action towards the elders

Guidance for Families from the Ramayana #14

Joint families are considered best for the upbringing of children. In such families, children learn calmness from their grandparents and about the pace of life from their parents. But joint-family structures have drastically reduced over time, due to urban jobs, lack of patience and miscommunication rife in modern lifestyles.

Grandparents have their own set of expectations, based on their belief systems. The current generations may find them unreasonable. In the olden times, everyone had their defined roles, unlike today, when an interchange of roles is very common and acceptable. These days, women in most households have jobs, so both parents work long hours to attain a desired standard of living. In such a fast-paced, multi-activity family system, casual family conversations inadvertently take a back seat.

Relationships based on communication, understanding, tolerance, patience and contribution are long-lasting. In modern times, ensuring one or two meals in a day together as a family and frequent simple family outings can become great opportunities to bond, communicate concerns, points of view and shrug off ego-related issues.

Bitterness occurs in relationships due to misunderstanding, assumptions, unreasonable expectations, impatience and lack of communication, as happened between Bali and Sugriva. Bali assumed that Sugriva had ill intentions but didn't bother to investigate or communicate before taking the severe action of banishing Sugriva out of the kingdom and taking his younger brother's wife disgracefully.

Family Reflection Time

Discuss with your family and share what kind of person you are. Do you have a habit of developing biases based on initial information, or do you attempt to clarify things through proper communication? You may want to note down your reflections, click a picture and share on social media with the hashtag #MyRamayana.

_____

_____

_____

_____

_____

_____

Idiom and Phrases from the Ramayana

Construct a sentence using the words 'classic Bali–Sugriva confusion'.

Example: Mamta and Rajkumari created an opinion about each other based on some rumours, which broke their friendship. It's such a classic Bali–Sugriva confusion.

_____

_____

_____

_____

_____

15

Logical Communication Can Win Battles: Learn How Rama Made Bali Realize His Folly

In the thoughtful win-win partnership between Rama and Sugriva, Rama promised Sugriva to assist him in getting his kingdom and wife, Ruma, back. Sugriva promised Rama that he would do whatever it took to search for Sita.

Rama took the lead in fulfilling his promise. He asked Sugriva to go and challenge Bali for a fight and planned to hide himself behind a tree, to eliminate Bali during the fight. But Bali and Sugriva looked so similar during the fight that Rama was not able to differentiate between them. Rama asked Sugriva to challenge Bali again, but this time he asked Sugriva to wear a distinctive garland as an identifier. When Bali and Sugriva were engaged in the brawl, Rama, hiding behind a tree, identified Bali clearly and launched an arrow at him. The next moment Bali was on the ground.

When Rama went near the dying Bali, with an arrow stuck in his chest, Bali asked Rama a few pertinent questions. First, Bali asked why the brave Rama had hidden himself behind a tree to attack him. Second: Why did Rama punish a non-guilty Bali. And third: Who was Rama to punish him, even if he was guilty? This conversation between the dying Bali and Rama is one of the most widely discussed episodes among Ramayana scholars.

Rama's logical replies to Bali were structured under three J's: justification, jurisprudence and jurisdiction. First, Rama justified his act of hiding behind a tree as a common hunting or war technique used by many to tackle an unpredictable enemy. Bali realized that he himself had used that strategy often. Then Rama reminded Bali of the great moral sin Bali had committed by keeping his younger brother's wife and pushing him away from the kingdom. Rama reminded Bali that he was like a father to Sugriva and Ruma was like his daughter-in-law. By misbehaving with Ruma, Bali had crossed all the boundaries of justice, tradition and virtue.

Rama's jurisprudence was completely clear and consistent. Rama further added that since he was a descendent of the Ikshvakus, the upholders of virtue and morality in society, he did not need any jurisdiction to punish anyone for such a heinous crime.

The dying Bali was convinced with Rama's answers. He realized the great sin he had committed and asked his wife, Tara, and son Angada to join Rama in his righteous mission.

Life Lesson #15 for Families

The dying Bali asked some sharp questions of Rama, and Rama's logical and rational replies embedded in the principles of justification, jurisprudence and jurisdiction satisfied even the dying Bali. This teaches us that:

> **Logical and rational communication can win battles for you.**

Family Scenario #15

Swarna and Pankaj have an adolescent boy named Yash, who is studying in grade nine. They observe that Yash has been spending a lot of time on digital devices for the past two years. The parents tried to be strict with Yash by saying a firm 'No' for prolonged use of these devices, forcefully taking the devices away as well as employing some other punitive methods. Though these methods solved the issue, they resulted in a lack of connection and trust between the parents and the child, and adversely affected Yash's performance in all areas of life. What, according to you, was wrong with the parents' approach?

A) The parents didn't try to understand the reasons for the child's increased dependence on gadgets by communicating
B) Yash didn't feel supported and understood by his parents, which resulted in poor parent–child connection
C) The parents used their authority to force their thoughts on Yash, rather than communicating and educating him logically and rationally

Guidance for Families from the Ramayana #15

In modern times, everyone is exposed to a multitude of digital devices and loads of digital information. If used effectively, digital mediums can open a new world of opportunities. But excessive use of digital means should be controlled. Due to the high level of stimulation offered by digital technology, it is very addictive in nature, not only for children but also for adults.

Controlling screen time and use of digital devices is a common concern among parents of children of all ages. It's worth the effort to explain to children, in a logical and rational manner, the 'what', 'why' and 'how' of the harms of excessive use of digital mediums—just like how Rama's logical and rational replies, embedded in the principles of justification, jurisprudence and jurisdiction, satisfied even the dying Bali.

Spending time with children to create a friendly bond with them, regularly going for simple outings, like jungle trails, bird-watching trails, trekking, visits to museums and historical monuments, etc., will immensely help children to connect the information available digitally to the real world.

Family Reflection Time

Bali's elimination at the hands of Rama is one of the most debated incidents of the Ramayana. Discuss your thoughts on the same with your family. You may want to note down your reflections, click a picture and share on social media with the hashtag **#MyRamayana**.

_____

_____

_____

_____

_____

_____

_____

_____

_____

Family Breakfast Discussion

Instead of partnering with the mighty king Bali, why did Rama plan to sort out Sugriva's problems first and then partner with him? Share your thoughts with your family.

_____

_____

_____

_____

_____

_____

_____

_____

_____

16

Motivation Can Do Wonders: How Jambavan Motivated Hanuman to Cross a Massive Sea

After Bali's death, Sugriva became the king of Kishkinda. Sugriva got his kingdom and his wife back. Rama had fulfilled his promise. Now it was Sugriva's turn to reciprocate. Back in the luxuries of the palace, Sugriva became slack and forgot his promise, only until the angry Laxmana shook him out of his slumber. Sugriva realized his mistake and made a comprehensive and strategic plan to search for Sita.

Sugriva constituted teams to go in the north, south, east and west directions to search for Mata Sita. Though the clues given by Jatayu and others pointed towards the south, Sugriva did not want to take any chance and decided to send the teams in all directions. But he sent the strongest team towards the south, comprising stalwarts like Jambavan, Hanuman, Nala, Nila, Angada and Tara. Yes, you read it right: Tara, Bali's wife. Women being part of armies is an old tradition of this land. Sugriva trained all the four teams meticulously and described the places they should search in their respective directions. His geographical descriptions for all four directions were so detailed that some scholars call them 'Sugriva's Atlas'.

The teams that went towards the north, east and west returned with no success. But the team sent to the south got stuck in an elusive cave, and when they managed to come out they found themselves in front of a massive sea. This place was Dhanushkodi, which is in today's Rameswaram Island of Ramanathapuram district of Tamil Nadu. The team was tired and disappointed. Angada was so ashamed of going back unsuccessful to Sugriva and Rama that he suggested mass suicide to everyone. Tara suggested that they all should live in that cave for the rest of their lives. In those moments of despair, Jambavan and Hanuman restored sanity in the team and started going over all the clues they had gathered from Rama and Laxmana. When they were discussing the clues given by Jatayu, one old bird from the eagle–vulture family, sitting on a rock near the sea, intervened and asked more about Jatayu. The bird identified himself as Sampathi and happened to be Jatayu's elder brother. When Sampathi heard about Jatayu's brave death, he too came forward to help in the search for Sita and gave two very crucial clues to the team. Pointing to a large island in front of them, Sampathi told the team that Ravana had taken Sita to that island and had kept her in Ashoka Vatika, a garden on the island.

The team that had lost all hopes felt rejuvenated. Now they had the final coordinates of Mata Sita. The challenge was to cross the sea—which was a hundred *yojanas*, i.e. a thousand miles wide—trace Sita and come back with the exact details. Old Jambavan started motivating the younger team members. Jambavan said that in his younger days he could have accomplished this task easily. Angada was the first one to offer to cross the sea but was unsure whether he was capable of coming back. When all this discussion was going on, Hanuman was sitting a little away from it all, contemplating. Jambavan, the wisest among all, knew about Hanuman's capabilities, which Hanuman had forgotten due to a curse in his childhood. Jambavan started reminding Hanuman about his outstanding capabilities, about his exceptional flying, jumping and swimming skills, and, most importantly, about his indomitable spirit of duty. Hanuman instantly responded to Jambavan's motivating discourse, regained his forgotten powers and got ready to cross the sea.

That concludes the Kishkinda Kanda.

Life Lesson #16 for Families

Jambavan's motivation reminded Hanuman of his forgotten skills and capabilities, and enabled him to cross a humongous sea. It's evident what the right motivation can do to people:

> Motivation can do wonders.

Family Scenario #16

Tanay is in the twelfth grade. He was born into a family of lawyers. He is fascinated with courtroom debates and wants to pursue the legal profession as a career. He knows that he has to appear for the Common Law Admission

Test (CLAT), which is one of the toughest exams in India to crack. This year, he has wasted almost three months due to sickness and is lagging behind even in his preparations for the twelfth-grade board exams. He has been getting suggestions from the elders around him, including parents, relatives and teachers. Which of the following statements do you think can help Tanay regain his motivation and confidence for the upcoming exams?

A) There is very little chance that you would do well in both CLAT and board exams, so focus only on one of them

B) You should attempt the board exams and CLAT with full vigour and energy; I am sure you will do well in the board exams and appearing for CLAT will be a good experience for you

C) I have seen you perform well when you are calm and focused; try to give your best in both exams

Guidance for Families from the Ramayana #16

Motivation is a major driving force behind human actions. Motivation directly correlates with prospects of success. As parents, it is important to keep our children motivated for learning. But can we really do it in a way that benefits them without putting them off? Can we create the right conditions and atmosphere that fosters motivation in them? Well, yes, of course, it is possible!

Motivating your child towards a goal is different from putting them under pressure and burdening them with unrealistic expectations. As parents, you know your child's potential well. You have to provide them with the right environment, where they can be calm, focused on their goal and perform the tasks at hand to the best of their ability. Motivation is the quintessential catalyst to enhance the performance of your child, as Jambavan motivated Hanuman to recollect his forgotten skills and capabilities.

Family Reflection Time

Can a mere motivational talk make someone complete a big task? Reflect on this and share your thoughts with the whole family. You may want to note down your reflections, click a picture and share on social media with the hashtag **#MyRamayana**.

_____

_____

_____

_____

_____

_____

_____

_____

Idiom and Phrases from the Ramayana

Construct a sentence using the words 'Jambavan-like motivation'.

Example: Reema failed the previous maths test even after preparing well for it. Now she needs Jambavan-like motivation to appear for the next test.

_____

_____

_____

_____

_____

_____

_____

_____

Your Favourite Character from the Kishkinda Kanda

Looking at the Kishkinda Kanda, we have learnt about various characters of the Ramayana. First, list all the characters in the Kishkinda Kanda. Then, thoughtfully choose the character you find most inspiring. Also, share why and how that character inspires you. Different family members may have different favourite characters. You may want to write down your thoughts about your favourite

character, click a photo and share on social media with the
hashtag **#MyRamayana**.

_____

_____

_____

_____

_____

_____

Kill the Ravana within You

At the end of the Kishkinda Kanda, let's take a moment
to identify our 'Rama' and 'Ravana' qualities again. Then
we should work to further strengthen our Rama qualities
and get rid of our Ravana qualities. You have already done
this exercise thrice before in the book. At this point, which
Ravanas within you do you want to eliminate? You may
want to jot down your answer, click a photo and share on
social media with the hashtag **#MyRamayana**.

_____

_____

_____

_____

_____

_____

Kishkinda Kanda Crossword Puzzle

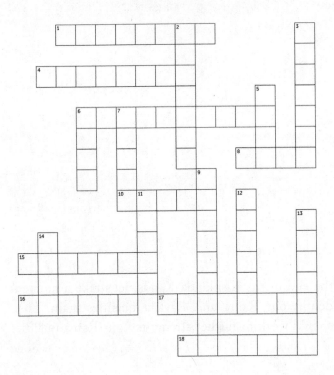

Find the answers on page 173

Across

1 _____ gave the clue that Mata Sita was across the sea

4 The head of the vanara army

6 The hill where Sugriva was hiding during his exile

8 Brother of Sugriva

10 Where is Hanuman's birthplace temple in the present times

15 He asks help from Rama to get his wife and kingdom

16 Ravana cuts his wing

17 The Asura brother of Mayavi

18 He gets angry with Sugriva for his inaction

Down

2 Rama and _____ became friends instantly

3 Gave Rama berries after tasting them

5 Wife of Bali

6 _____ kills Bali

7 The strongest team sent to the _____ for the search of Sita

9 Sugriva and Bali ruled

11 Son of Bali

12 Sampathi's brother

13 The vanara king

14 Wife of Sugriva

PART V

Sundar Kanda[*]
Value of Trust and Judgement

---

[*] Sundar refers to beautiful, handsome, virtuous and good.

17

Don't Celebrate Too Early:
As Hanuman Teaches Us

With Jambavan's motivational therapy, Hanuman took off for Lanka in search of Mata Sita. In the middle of the sea was the Mainaka Mountain. It enticed Hanuman, offering that he rest for a while on his strenuous journey across the sea. But Hanuman swore by the divine task Rama had bestowed on him and continued on his mission without any rest. Then came demoness Surasa to  obstruct his way. With his wit and agility, Hanuman outsmarted her and moved on. Overcoming many such obstructions and hindrances, he finally reached Lanka. He was awestruck seeing the beautiful, magnificent, golden city of Lanka, designed by none other than the master architect Vishwakarma.

Hanuman was super happy and excited to have completed his arduous journey and reached Lanka in his search for Sita. He had accomplished a major task for his beloved Rama. He thought that now it was just a matter of time before he traced Mata Sita on this small island. But his happiness was short-lived. When he gave a close and serious look to the heavily guarded 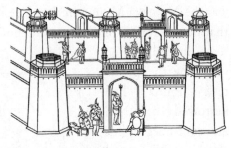 Lanka at one side and the humongous sea on the other, two very strategic challenges emerged in his mind, and his excitement rested for a while. First, the city of Lanka seemed extremely tough to get into, as it was heavily guarded by demon soldiers. Second, the sea was huge. Getting Sugriva's army to cross the sea and come to Lanka to wage a war against Ravana seemed to be a daunting task.

Hanuman soon realized that his premature excitement, just on crossing the sea alone, was quite misplaced.

Life Lesson #17 for Families

Hanuman was excited to have crossed the sea and reached Lanka, and started celebrating it as a victory. But soon, he realized that Lanka was heavily guarded and not easy to get into. He also realized that getting Sugriva's entire army to cross the sea would be a huge challenge. So he quickly recalibrated his early excitement and got back to the task. This incident teaches us:

> **Don't celebrate too early.**

Family Scenario #17

Mahesh's daughter Varada won the intermediate stage of the national archery championship. She seemed quite ahead in the tally. She was very happy and confident that she would win the final competition, and organized a party with family and friends. She started avoiding the practice schedule that she used to follow. What should be Mahesh's thought process in this situation in the best interests of his daughter?

A) Mahesh should appreciate her for her achievement and support her non-serious attitude and overconfidence with the belief that she will definitely win

B) Mahesh should appreciate her for her achievement and be happy, without much concern for her further performance
C) Mahesh should not appreciate her so soon and ask her to practise for the next level
D) Mahesh should appreciate her and ask her to practise harder and strategically for the next level; he should counsel her regarding the importance of continuing to focus on reaching the final destination

Guidance for Families from the Ramayana #17

There are many instances when you are almost confident that the job will be done according to your satisfaction, but something unexpected comes up and spoils the outcome. Celebrating things before they are fully complete makes us complacent. When you celebrate too early you tend to lose focus on your goal. And on the flip side, don't give up too early either, because tables can always turn if you keep trying—just as the Vanara team towards the south did not give up, and Hanuman realized his mistake of rejoicing and celebrating too soon and recalibrated his early excitement, getting back to the task.

Family Reflection Time

Share some personal incidents with your family where you might have celebrated too early and faced embarrassment and disappointment later. You may want to note down your reflections, click a picture and share on social media with the hashtag **#MyRamayana**.

Family Breakfast Discussion

Search videos of sporting events on the Internet, where celebrating too early became the reason for failure for sportspersons at the highest level.

18

Learn from Your Mistakes: Check How Sita Got Doubly Cautious after One Mistake

Hanuman eliminated Lankini* to enter into Lanka. Now, the next task was to trace Mata Sita.

He carefully started scanning from street to street, house to house, palace to palace, to find Sita. He encountered many women—some dancing, some singing, chanting hymns, cooking, resting, etc. But no one matched the grace and divinity of Sita, as described in detail by Rama to Hanuman. By now, Hanuman was hungry, and his body was extremely tired after crossing the humongous sea. But he kept his search on.

To grab some fruits to re-energize himself, he reached a garden. Coincidentally, there he saw a lady sitting quietly. She looked out of sorts but determined nonetheless. Her

---

* Lankini guarded the doors of Lanka.

grace and aura matched with Rama's description of Sita. Hanuman hid himself behind a nearby tree and started observing her.

At the same moment, a ferocious demon approached Sita. With all the kingly protocols surrounding the demon, Hanuman guessed it was Ravana. And indeed, he was Ravana. Ravana addressed Sita with contempt and forcibly asked her to marry him. Sita did not even look at Ravana. Looking away, Sita suggested that Ravana should apologize to her husband, Rama, and return her to Rama. She warned Ravana of the dire consequences of keeping her in captivity in Lanka. She predicted doomsday for the whole of Lanka and the Asura clan at the hands of Rama. Sita displayed unprecedented courage and character by challenging Ravana in his kingdom, in his captivity, surrounded by his demons. A rattled Ravana gave two months' ultimatum to Sita and gave her two choices—either to marry him or become his breakfast after two months.

By hearing the whole conversation, Hanuman was certain
that the woman was Sita. Sitting on the tree, he started
singing the story of Rama in a melodious voice, which
caught Sita's attention. He came down, introduced
himself to Sita as Rama's messenger and told her about
Rama's well-being and whereabouts. Sita was hearing
some pleasant news after many months. All this while in
Ravana's captivity, she was certain that Rama would trace
her. Her undying hope kept her afloat. But on second
thought, she felt the presence of Rama's messenger too
good to be true. Hanuman narrated many incidents of
Rama. Sita wanted to trust Hanuman, but she had also
learnt from her grave mistake of misjudging Ravana when
he had come in the guise of a saint. She understood the
thin line between trusting and carefully judging a person
or a situation.

Sita asked Hanuman to further prove his identity. Sita asked Hanuman to assure her that he was not an elusive demon in the form of Rama's messenger. Hanuman and Rama had already anticipated this. They knew that after the Ravana incident, Sita would not trust anyone easily. So Rama gave his ring to Hanuman as a passcode to prove his identity in front of Sita. As soon as Hanuman showed Rama's ring to Sita, she was in tears and was sure of Hanuman's close bond with her husband. Sita and Hanuman also knew that Rama might not readily believe that

Hanuman had met the real Sita, given the illusion of spells cast by demons and demonesses. So Sita gave her hairclip, the *Chudamani*, to Hanuman as a counter passcode, so that Rama could ascertain that Hanuman had met the real Sita.

Life Lesson #18 for Families

Sita was tricked by Ravana when she blindly trusted him in the disguise of a saint. With Hanuman, she did not repeat the mistake and ascertained his identity beyond doubt before trusting him as Rama's messenger.

> **Learn from your mistakes. There is a thin line between trust and judgement.**

Family Scenario #18

Saurabh is in ninth grade and is afraid of making friends in school. In the seventh grade, he had made the mistake of befriending Rahul, just by observing his expensive lifestyle—luxury cars with drivers to drop him off, foreign chocolates as giveaways every week, branded school bags, expensive holidays, etc. Later, the same Rahul mischievously framed Saurabh in a fight between some classmates. Saurabh felt betrayed and stopped making friends. As parents, how will you bring Saurabh out of his bad experience?

A) By asking him to make friends with students of the same economic status
B) By guiding him to learn from his mistakes and make a nuanced judgement before trusting anyone
C) By guiding him that in the modern world no one can be trusted and telling him that he has to be watchful

Guidance for Families from the Ramayana #18

There's a thin line between trust and judgement. We make friends based on outer appearances, clothes, their way of talking, etc. That's absolutely normal. Rich and poor, all can be great friends—there is no standard pattern there. One should not become cynical on account of one faulty selection of a friend and stop trusting people. Learning from your mistakes makes your instincts sharper for future decisions. Sita learnt from her mistake in the Ravana incident and then doubly checked Hanuman's credentials before trusting him.

By looking back at what actually happened and what you could have done differently, you turn a mistake into a set-up for success. Admit the mistake to yourself or to the person affected by it, so you can re-examine how things happened and do better the next time. If facing your errors makes you anxious or frightened, remind yourself how normal this is. Every single person makes mistakes. Most failures are temporary setbacks, rather than absolute disasters. People who achieve great things often had great failures along the way.

Family Reflection Time

Share an incident with your family where you learnt a big life lesson from your mistake. You may want to note down your reflections, click a picture and share on social media with the hashtag #MyRamayana.

_____

_____

_____

_____

_____

_____

_____

_____

Family Breakfast Discussion

Do you sometimes feel the need to apply your judgement even on the people and things you trust? Discuss some real-life cases with family members.

_____

_____

_____

_____

_____

_____

_____

19

Evaluate Your Strengths and Weaknesses before Battle: Learn How Hanuman Did It Effectively

By tracing Mata Sita, ensuring it was the real Sita and, in turn, establishing his true identity as the messenger of Rama, Hanuman had accomplished a big milestone in his 'Search of Sita' mission. But Hanuman was not one of those who would just accomplish what was assigned to them. He had a larger vision. He knew that the whole army of Sugriva would soon come to Lanka. He wanted to keep the intelligence ready for them. He wanted to know the topography of Lanka, its strengths, weaknesses and more about its king, Ravana.

To fix his tryst with Ravana, Hanuman came up with a ploy. He started creating havoc at the Ashoka Vatika, the garden where Sita was confined. He started uprooting trees and throwing them on the demon guards in the garden. Word went to Ravana's court, and he sent an army to counter Hanuman. The team came back beaten black and blue. Then Ravana sent his son Akshay Kumar to tame Hanuman. Akshay Kumar was no match for Hanuman and got killed in countering him. Then Ravana had no option but to send his elder son Indrajeet. After the initial battle, Indrajeet realized that Hanuman was not an ordinary warrior. Indrajeet had to launch the Brahmastra[*] to capture Hanuman. Hanuman bowed down out of respect for the Brahmastra, and happily allowed himself to be captured and taken to Ravana's court.

At Ravana's court, Hanuman identified himself as Rama's messenger. He advised Ravana to ask for Rama's forgiveness and return Mata Sita if he wanted to stop the destruction of Lanka and the Asura clan. A rattled Ravana ordered his soldiers to capture and kill Hanuman. In the *adharmic*[†] court of Ravana, there was a sole sane voice: his younger brother Vibhishana. Vibhishana warned Ravana and the court that it was against the rules of the court to kill any messenger. On Vibhishana's advice, Ravana refrained from killing Hanuman but ordered his soldiers to set Hanuman's tail on fire.

By virtue of Sita Mata's prayer to Goddess Agni, the fire did not harm Hanuman. But using his fired tail as a torch, Hanuman burnt down almost one-third of Lanka. And in the smoke and mayhem, Hanuman did a thorough recce of Lanka and assessed its strong and weak points. Through this act, Hanuman also gave a clear signal to

---

[*] Brahmastra was an arrow with special powers.
[†] Adharmic refers to being non-righteous in this context.

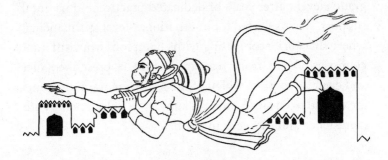

Ravana and his army that if a messenger could do such damage to Lanka and Asuras, they should imagine and fear what the whole army of Sugriva could do.

And that concludes Sundar Kanda.

Life Lesson #19 for Families

Hanuman turned the tables in Lanka. When Ravana's soldiers set Hanuman's tail on fire, Hanuman used his tail as a torch and burnt a large part of Lanka. In the confusion caused by the smoke, Hanuman also assessed the strengths and weaknesses of Lanka and its army, to provide crucial intelligence to his side.

> Evaluate your and your opponents' strengths and weaknesses.

Family Scenario #19

Samiksha, daughter of Kiran and Anu, has been a badminton player since the fourth grade in school. By grade eleven, after years of dedicated practice and parental support, she is selected for international-level tournaments, where she will be competing with champions from different countries. Apart from regular practice, a prescribed diet and exercise routine, which of the following training points are crucial to ensure Samiksha appears in tournaments with confidence and succeeds in them?

A) Watch the videos of all opponents and keenly observe their strengths and weaknesses
B) Keep a close watch on her own strengths and weaknesses, with the help of her coach
C) All of the above

Guidance for Families from the Ramayana #19

In those sports where you have to play against an opponent, apart from keeping tabs on your own game, carefully assessing the opponent's game is also crucial. For example, in badminton, you should, on the one hand, play to your strengths and cover up your weak areas, and, on the other hand, you should exploit the weaknesses of your opponent. Doing a SWOT analysis, meaning the analysis of strengths, weaknesses, opportunities and threats, in relation to yourself and your opponents, is a worthwhile exercise to be in the control of the situation. Hanuman's conduct during his Lanka visit is a great example of this.

Family Reflection Time

Share an incident with your family where evaluating the strengths and weaknesses of the opponent helped you go through a complicated situation. You may want to note down your reflections, click a picture and share on social media with the hashtag **#MyRamayana**.

_____

_____

_____

_____

_____

Family Breakfast Discussion

SWOT analysis is a well-established management principle in modern times for organizational assessment. Do you think it is relevant at the family level too? Discuss with your family.

_____

_____

_____

_____

_____

Your Favourite Character from the Sundar Kanda

In the Sundar Kanda, we have learnt about various characters of the Ramayana. First, list all the characters in the Sundar Kanda. Then thoughtfully choose the character you find most inspiring. Also, share why and how that character inspires you. Different family members may have different favourite characters. You may want to note down your thoughts about your favourite character, click a photo and share on social media with the hashtag **#MyRamayana**.

_____

_____

_____

_____

_____

_____

_____

_____

Kill the Ravana Within You

At the end of the Sundar Kanda, let's take a moment to identify our 'Rama' and 'Ravana' qualities again. Then we should work to further strengthen our Rama qualities and get rid of our Ravana qualities. You have already done this exercise a few times before in the book. At this point, which

Ravanas within you do you want to eliminate? How are they different from the previous Ravanas that you had listed? You may want to jot down your answer, click a picture and share on social media with the hashtag **#MyRamayana**.

_____

_____

_____

_____

_____

_____

_____

_____

Sundar Kanda Crossword Puzzle

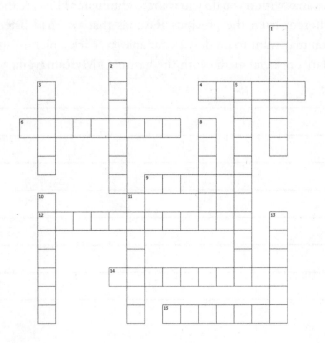

Across

4 Lanka Naresh

6 Meghnad was also known as_____

9 Hanuman's mother

12 Where mata Sita was kept in Lanka

14 Ravana's brother who joined Rama's army

15 Hanuman checked out the whole of Lanka sitting on _____ hill

Down

1 Mighty mountain that obstructed Hanuman on his way to Lanka

2 The rakshasi who guarded Sita in Lanka

3 Ravana ruled _____

5 Architect of Lanka

8 Hanuman's father

10 Pavan putra _____

11 The rakshasi who guarded the doors of Lanka

13 Goddess of the serpents

Find the answers on page 173

PART VI

Yudha Kanda[*]
Don't Be Surrounded by Yes-Men

---

[*] Yudha means war.

20

Stay Away from Yes-Men: Ravana Was Surrounded by Them

Hanuman returned victorious from Lanka. But he left a burnt Lanka and an angry Ravana behind. Ravana wanted to kill Hanuman in his court, but Vibhishana stopped him. After Hanuman left, Vibhishana advised his elder brother Ravana to return Sita to Rama and make peace with him. Vibhishana advised Ravana against the war. Vibhishana flagged Ravana's inappropriate act of kidnapping someone's wife and putting the whole Asura clan at risk to defend this act of utmost immorality.

Ravana surely did not like Vibhishana's advice. Instead of returning Sita, he forced Vibhishana to leave Lanka. Ravana told Vibhishana that no one could sing his enemy Rama's praise in his court. Ravana doubted Vibhishana's loyalty towards Lanka and its crown, and ordered him to leave Lanka. In his fit of rage, Ravana also advised Vibhishana to side with Rama and be known as a traitor for life.

Vibhishana was not the first one who advised Ravana against the war with Rama. Maricha was the first one to bell the cat. When Ravana had asked Maricha to help him in kidnapping Sita by becoming the golden deer, Maricha had warned Ravana against it. Maricha had said that he had first-hand experience of facing the meticulous war skills of Rama and Laxmana. Maricha narrated how Rama and Laxmana, while protecting Sage Vishwamitra's yagna, killed his mother, brother and fellow demons, and how he himself had escaped their arrows narrowly. Maricha further warned that Rama–Laxmana had been deadly in their teens when he first encountered them, and by now they were far better trained and fierce warriors. He had vehemently discouraged Ravana from kidnapping Sita but had later succumbed to his king's order and lost his life to Rama in the process. Later, Ravana's head queen, Mandodari, also tried hard to persuade him to free Sita. Malyavan, Ravana's maternal grandfather, a trusted counsel for Ravana, advised Ravana against the war. Kumbhkaran, when woken up for the war, also didn't like the idea of kidnapping a woman and defending this wrong action through a war. Sita, Hanuman and Angada, from Rama's side, had tried to put similar sense in Ravana's head. But Ravana did not give heed to any of them.

Ravana was happy with a bunch of war-hungry yes-men around him. His sons, his army chiefs and his court men all kept boosting Ravana's ego.

Life Lesson #20 for Families

The day Ravana planned to kidnap Sita, he started walking on the path of complete destruction of the Asuras. He was blinded by his motive. Many of his friends and relatives tried hard to alarm him, but Ravana listened only to his yes-men and faced the consequences.

> **Stay away from yes-men.**

Family Scenario #20

Ajay was the sales head of a large automobile company in north India. He was smooth with his conversation skills and good at convincing people. He used his skills to his advantage. But lately, his wife, Surabhi, noticed an aberration in Ajay's normal, hard-working routine. To meet his sales target, he had started using unscrupulous ways, started selling false promises, started siding with notorious brokers of the trade. When Surabhi tried to point this out,

Ajay shrugged her off disrespectfully. Ajay's usual circle of friends, well-wishers and colleagues also changed over time. He was not ready to hear any criticism of his new, easy way of selling. What will be your advice for Ajay?

A) If success is coming your way, the means are not so important
B) Keep with you a few friends from whom you are ready to take critical feedback
C) Take everyone's advice, but do whatever you wish to do

Guidance for Families from the Ramayana #20

Everyone likes their ideas to be praised and endorsed. We are all in love with our ideas and even constructive feedback can sound like criticism. But feedback can always help improve your idea and make it robust. In fact, one should always consult a set of experts to critically thrash one's ideas and make them more effective. Many times, we like to create an echo chamber around us and gather people who get paid to praise us. These yes-men may sound very comforting to us, but they praise us to retain their jobs rather than to help us improve. Ravana's yes-men insulated him from all the wise opinions coming from Maricha, Vibhishana, Mandodari and others, and became the prime reason for his demise.

Family Reflection Time

Share an incident with your family where a group of yes-men around you boosted your ego but pushed you into a doomed situation. You may want to note down your reflections, click a picture and share on social media with the hashtag **#MyRamayana**.

_____

_____

_____

_____

_____

_____

_____

Family Breakfast Discussion

There is a famous couplet by the Indian poet and saint Kabir in a similar context, 'Nindak Niyare Rakhiye . . .' Look up the complete couplet and discuss it with your family.

_____

_____

_____

_____

_____

_____

21

Value Your Team Members as Rama Did

Ousted from Lanka, Vibhishana had no option but to side with righteousness, propriety and dharma. It was a huge dilemma for Vibhishana to part ways from his brother Ravana and explore the possibility of joining Rama. Vibhishana approached Rama along with his close aides and expressed his desire to stand with Rama in the war. For Vibhishana, Rama was the embodiment of dharma.

Now, Rama's dilemma was whether to trust Vibhishana and make him a part of the team. He did not decide about this alone. He was a true team player. He called all his trusted team members and asked each of them for their views. Rama realized that his team had two sets of opinions. Many team members, led by Sugriva, were against the idea of Vibhishana joining the team. They feared the possibility of Vibhishana being a mole planted by Ravana to get their war secrets. But Hanuman endorsed Vibhishana's joining the team, as Vibhishana was the sole dharmic voice Hanuman had found in Ravana's adharmic court during his Lanka visit. Rama weighed the fact that Hanuman was arguing from personal experience, while others were invoking war strategies. Rama was also cognizant of the fact that apart from Hanuman, no one in his team had first-hand experience of the Lankan terrain.

Rama needed someone local who had a good understanding of Ravana's army, his war strategies, his strengths and weaknesses, and Lanka's geography. Hanuman's word carried weight, and so Rama decided to accept Vibhishana in his team.

Life Lesson #21 for Families

Unlike Ravana, who only heard his yes-men, Rama valued his team members.

> **Value your team members and value local leadership.**

Family Scenario #21

Narahari and his wife, Shobhna, are reaching seventy years of age now. They have lived a fulfilling life in a joint family. Narahari's brothers and their children, all live together in a two-storey building. They all live together on the first and second floors of their parental house. Rental money from the ground-floor shops helps the whole big family with their expenses. Now, taking the stairs to the second floor multiple times a day is painful for both Narahari and Shobhna. They have started contemplating shifting to a rented house on the ground floor or to some other house with elevators. They acted as moral leaders for the whole big family for so many years. The children of the house look up to them. Their absence will be felt by everyone. How should they plan their move to the new place?

A) It's their life and they should do whatever is most comfortable for them
B) They should convince everyone in the family to move together to a more convenient house
C) They should discuss with everyone in the family, share their concern and reach a collective solution

Guidance for Families from the Ramayana #21

Narahari and Shobhna have decided to move to a new and more comfortable house because of their old age. They played the role of captains for the whole joint family for many years. All family members seek their advice and approval for many decisions in their lives. Their moving out will leave a void in the family. It will be great if Narahari and Shobhna gather the whole family, old and young, and share their problem, about how difficult they find walking up the stairs. Many solutions may come up with consultation. Maybe there's an engineering solution too—of installing an elevator in the old house. Maybe they all can sell or rent the old house and move to a modern house. Maybe the young ones in the family can suggest good rental houses nearby with elevators, so that they both live in proximity to the whole family. Learning from how Rama valued his team members can be a beautiful asset in this case too.

Family Reflection Time

Do you treat and consider your family as a cohesive team and value the opinion of each member of the team? Share your thoughts with your family. You may want to jot down your reflections, click a picture and share on social media with the hashtag **#MyRamayana**.

_____

_____

_____

_____

_____

_____

_____

Family Breakfast Discussion

How has your family used local knowledge and leadership
of friends and relatives to its advantage? Discuss among
your family members.

_____

_____

_____

_____

_____

_____

_____

22

You Need Merit and Power for Any Negotiation: On Rama's Prowess

How will the whole army cross the sea to reach Lanka? Hanuman had anticipated this problem before anyone else. The sea was the biggest moat, saving Ravana's Lanka for attacks. Even Vibhishana did not have any advice for Rama to solve this deadlock.

Rama decided to pray and earnestly request the sea to provide him and his army a way to reach Lanka for his dharmic mission. 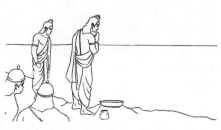 Rama prayed meticulously, with folded hands. But even after such a diligent request, when the sea did not appear to heed his request, Rama decided to leave the requesting mode. Rama told Laxmana that the sea seemed to be considering him as an incapable man because of his patience and soft attitude. Rama further added that in this world, it is not possible to obtain victory only by conciliation. He said that it would be a mistake to keep showing forbearance to the sea.

Rama knew that it was the time to show his prowess. Not only wars but even negotiations can be won from a position of strength. Rama told Laxmana that the sea did not seem to be interested in his kind words, and asked Laxmana to bring his bow and serpentine arrows, so that he could dry up the sea and his army could cross it by foot. Rama lifted his bow and, making the earth tremble, released a powerful arrow. His sharp arrows penetrated the waters of the sea, striking the inhabitants of the sea with terror. Thousands of mountain-sized waves jumped up from the sea, with all its inhabitants—crocodiles, snakes and others—making loud noises.

When Rama was about to release his next powerful arrow, the Sea God appeared in person before him with folded hands  and apologized for his non-appearance earlier. He argued that flowing was his natural dharma, and he could stop flowing. The Sea God advised Rama to get a bridge constructed across the sea. One of the members of the Vanara army, Nala, could do that. So Nala constructed a bridge across the sea with the help of Neel and other members of the Vanara army.

Life Lesson #22 for Families

The sea did not care about Rama's request as long as Rama had maintained a soft demeanour. The sea did not agree to negotiate until Rama showed his prowess. Enter every negotiation from the position of power. This incident teaches us that:

> **You need merit and power to win any negotiation.**

Family Scenario #22

Abhilasha and Shekhar are finding it difficult lately to negotiate the terms of the daily routine of their adolescent son, Sandeep. This is seriously impacting the functioning of the family, and they have been unable to meet the desired goals. Sandeep's lack of responsibility, refusal to take ownership and willingness to be distracted are getting out of control for the parents to manage. They take professional help, and the counsellor tells them that the parents' work schedule, as well as their negotiation tactics and overpromising on sales calls (overheard by the child) are having an effect on the child. What do you think may be the reasons for the non-compliant attitude of children towards their parents?

A) Parents are not able to present themselves as role models
B) Children take their parents' erratic behaviour as an excuse for such aberrations in their own attitude
C) Parents are unable to negotiate with the child, as they themselves are arguing from a position of weakness

Guidance for Families from the Ramayana #22

Every parent wants their child to perform well in studies, follow a good routine, eat healthy food and imbibe good values. Parents constantly negotiate with their children on these counts in their own ways. But these negotiations and persuasions become weak and ineffective when parents are unable to project themselves as role models on these counts. Exhibiting model behaviour is the best way of parenting. If a child constantly observes you making false promises on calls, your erratic lifestyle, your refrigerator full of unhealthy food, it will be very difficult for you to negotiate your desired terms with your child. Like Rama, you have to enter even the smallest of family negotiations from a position of power to expect positive outcomes.

23

Common Sense Is Not So Common: Hanuman's Common Sense Saved Many Lives

The Rama Setu was built across the ocean under the guidance of Nala and Neel, and the whole Vanara army reached Lanka. Rama's war skills had grown sharper over the thirteen years of his exile. He had learnt essential

lessons on warcraft from various sages and experts. He had absorbed valuable inputs from Vibhishana, Hanuman, Sugriva, Jambavan and others. So Rama strategically placed his army at the four gates of Lanka. He, along with Laxmana, led the army towards the northern gate of Lanka, which was guarded by Ravana himself.

Rama was still not in favour of war. He knew that war would cause destruction. He made one last attempt at truce by sending Angada as his messenger of peace.  Angada tried his best to convince Ravana, but in vain. In fact, Ravana commanded his soldiers to seize Angada. Bali's son Angada shook away the soldiers who tried to seize him, ascended to the roof of Ravana's palace, trampled and crushed it down by his strength, and returned to his camp. Hanuman and Angada had given enough hints to Ravana about Rama and his army's strength. But Ravana seemed blinded by his vicious motive.

Eventually, the war started between the two armies. Ravana's son Indrajit gave the first blow to the opposition camp by wounding Rama and Laxmana, who fell unconscious, injured by his serpentine arrows. Garuda, king of the birds, came to the rescue and set them free from the serpentine bondage. Following this incident, Rama's men mounted a full-throttle assault. Soon, Ravana found that the best of his army heads were dead—Dhoomraksha,

Vajradamshtra, Akampana and Prahasta. This was followed by the demise of his beloved sons Trishira, Narantaka, Mahodara, Atikaya and Devantaka. Akshay Kumar had been eliminated by Hanuman even before the war. And Ravana had lost five more sons.

Ravana was devastated by now. His son Indrajit and brother Kumbhkaran were the only warriors of stature Ravana was left with. Kumbhkaran was woken up to be sent for the war. He didn't approve of the idea of kidnapping Sita, but he complied with his brother eventually. Kumbhkaran created quite a havoc on the battlefield, but even he was eliminated. Rama himself had to come to the battlefield to finish him.

Indrajit was the only option left now with Ravana. Indrajit promised his father that he would destroy Rama and Laxmana. Indrajit, the ferocious son of Ravana, launched himself on the battlefield with full intensity. He used his magical and elusive tricks to deceive the opposition. Indrajit then showered a multitude of arrows on the army, which was almost like a big explosion, in which a large part of the army fell unconscious, including Rama and Laxmana.

Hanuman, Vibhishana and Jambavan were the only ones who were conscious among the senior members of Rama's team. Jambavan advised Hanuman to go to the Himalayas quickly to bring four important herbs: Mrita

Sanjivani, Vishalya Karani, Suvarna Karani and Sandhani. Hanuman began his journey to the Himalayas and reached Mount Rishabha, where the wonderful herbs were. Though Jambavan had given quite detailed descriptions of the herbs to Hanuman, many herbs, to Hanuman's surprise, seemed similar in appearance. Hanuman did not have much time to decide. He did not have the luxury to verify which herbs were the right ones with Jambavan, as he was almost 3000 kilometres away.

He was also mindful of the fact that many members of his army had fainted and needed large  quantities of herbs to get well. So he used common sense and unearthed a large piece of mountain, with all its herbs, and carried it back to his teammates. Inhaling those herbs, Rama, Laxmana and all the other members of the army regained their health.

Life Lesson #23 for Families

Hanuman shows his acumen multiple times in the Ramayana. In the Himalayas, when he was not able to identify the exact set of herbs and did not have means and time to verify the herbs with Jambavan, he did not resort to any complex solutions. He did not waste time either. He just used common sense. He used his brute strength and took a large piece of the mountain with plenty of herbs to the battlefield.

Common sense is *not* so common.

Family Scenario #23

Ekta and Tushar's son Sushant is travelling alone out of the city for the first time. The three of them had travelled widely over the last many years. Sushant had a decent idea about hotels, taxis, airports, bus stands, train stations, etc. But this time, as he is travelling alone, he is a little nervous. He goes up to his parents to ask for advice for his first solo trip. What advice should they give him?

A) They should advise him to be alert and not talk to strangers
B) They should advise him to draw on his travel experience from previous family trips and use common sense as per the situation
C) They should advise him to make all the travel and accommodation arrangements in advance

Guidance for Families from the Ramayana #23

Learning from travelling is quite valuable. Anyone who gets the opportunity to travel early in life is fortunate. Parents should ensure that travel becomes an integral part of the upbringing of their children. Travel instils respect for coexistence, teaches how to manage things using available resources, develops appreciation for different cultures, food, languages, etc., and makes you spontaneous and gives you the aptitude whereby you use common sense instead of complex solutions. Being paranoid of people and situations during travel will kill the fun of the trip and the learning you can get from it. If Sushant already has extensive experience of travel with his family, he has already, unconsciously, developed common sense for his upcoming solo trip.

Family Reflection Time

Share an incident with your family where your application of common sense saved everyone from a big problem. You may want to jot down your reflections, click a picture and share on social media with the hashtag **#MyRamayana**.

_____

_____

_____

_____

_____

_____

_____

Family Breakfast Discussion

How does one develop common sense? Share your thoughts
with your family members.

_____

_____

_____

_____

_____

_____

_____

24

In the Longer Run, the Truthful One Wins: Rama's Perseverance Paid Off

After regaining health, Laxmana vowed to eliminate Indrajit before he completed the sacrificial fire in the sanctuary of Nikumbhila, to earn more power. A fierce archery battle started between Indrajit and Laxmana, and the latter came out triumphant. Now Ravana was by himself. All his army heads, sons and brothers had been eliminated by Rama and his team.

Finally, Ravana came to the battlefield himself to confront Rama. Rama got a worthy adversary in the form of Ravana—not only in skill but also in wisdom. Ravana was a scholar of the Vedas and an ardent follower of Lord Shiva. His deep penance to Lord Shiva had earned him multiple powers and weapons. He was a noted musician of his times—the one who composed the famous Shiv Tandav Stotram.* He was a great chemist and had developed

---

* Shiv Tandav Stotram is a famous religious composition.

techniques to derive from herbs their essence. He was a maverick engineering brain and had reverse-engineered the Pushpaka Vimana and developed many other aircraft. He designed a game similar to today's chess and used to play it in his spare time. Ravana was not an ordinary opponent. It was a clash of the titans that the whole universe was waiting to watch.

Ravana was at a strategic height, as he was attacking from his Pushpaka Vimana. So Lord Indra sent his chariot for Rama, to make it a level playing field. Both started showering the deadliest of missiles in the form of arrows at each other. Sometimes it was an advantage to Rama and sometimes to Ravana. The two warriors shook up the whole earth. The entire earth, including mountains, groves and forests, trembled. The sun became gloomy, and the wind stopped blowing. When Rama cut off Ravana's head, another head cropped up in its place. The fierce encounter continued thus for seven days.

For a moment, Rama doubted that his fierce arrows—which had killed Maricha, Khara, Dushana, Kabandha and Viradha in Dandaka forest, and by which seven sala trees and whole mountains had been destroyed, by which undefeatable Bali had been killed and the sea shaken up—might not be effective against Ravana.

Then, the valiant Rama was reminded by his charioteer, Matali, of the hissing, serpent-like Brahmastra weapon given to him by the glorious sage Agastya. That arrow had the efficacy of a thunderbolt and capacity of tearing off entire armies of adversaries in battlefields. The arrow pierced Ravana's chest and then penetrated the earth.

The mighty Ravana was dead. Rama and his Vanara army had won over the mighty army of Lanka. After fourteen gruelling years, Rama had emerged as a winner. Fourteen years back, he had been exiled from his kingdom just a day before being anointed as the king. When he was about to complete the exile his wife got kidnapped. And fighting the war to get his wife back, he came very close to losing his life, twice. Though he had lost his kingdom, and almost lost his wife and his life, he never lost his goodness and his sense of propriety. He did not lose his wisdom. He did not take shortcuts. He did not use any inappropriate means to win the war. He did not leave his Vanvasa* dharma even for a day during those fourteen challenging years of exile. He did not run back to his brother Bharata for help. He made local allies and won the war against the mighty Ravana.

The death of the negativity called Ravana is celebrated as Dussehra across India.

Life Lesson #24 for Families

Whenever you are in trouble or feeling anxious, just think of Rama's journey of fourteen years, where he suffered so many setbacks. But his perseverance paid off, and in the end, the good, the honest and the truthful Rama won.

> **In the long run, the good, the honest and the truthful one wins.**

Family Scenario #24

Abhishek is among the toppers in his class. He has noticed that some of his classmates who were ahead of him in rank had cheated and got extra marks. This disappoints him immensely. As parents, what will you advise Abhishek?

---

* Vanvasa means exile in jungle.

A) He should do whatever it takes to excel in exams
B) He should complain to the teachers about the students who cheat
C) He should be consistent with his truthful ways of learning about his subjects and writing exams

Guidance for Families from the Ramayana #24

Exams and grades at school are one of the factors that determine future college admissions and placements. But every college conducts their own entrance test for admissions, and every company conducts its own series of rounds for selection. Most entrance exams are computer-adaptive now, and there is hardly any scope of cheating. If Abhishek studies well and makes his grasp of concepts strong, it will only help him in the long run to crack the entrance tests of colleges and companies. As parents, you should guide your children that cheating is a shortcut that may look lucrative in the short term but does not yield long-term results. Whenever one is disappointed in life, he or she should think of the challenges that Rama faced during his exile and how he overcame them with his perseverance, honesty and truthfulness.

Family Reflection Time

Share an incident with your family where your honesty and perseverance finally paid off. You may want to note down your reflections, click a picture and share on social media with the hashtag #MyRamayana.

_____

_____

_____

_____

_____

_____

_____

Family Breakfast Discussion

What's your primary and fundamental learning from the Ramayana? Every member should share their set of learnings.

_____

_____

_____

_____

_____

_____

_____

25

Do You Want to Be Rama or Ravana?

Ravana was not just another enemy. He was a meritorious man. He was a man of skills and virtues. He was also a renowned scholar. The ten heads signify his knowledge of the six shastras and the four Vedas. Lord Shiva was pleased with Ravana's penance and offered him a boon. Ravana asked for supremacy over gods, wild animals, rakshasas and other spirits. However, in his arrogance, he did not ask for protection from mortal human beings. Eventually, he met his end at the hands of a human. Ravana's ego destroyed him and his clan.

Rama, too, earned his skills and spiritual powers under revered gurus. But Rama used his powers and kingly lineage to help and uplift people. We have seen how Rama conducted himself with Guha, Jatayu, Shabri, exiled king Sugriva and Vibhishana. Rama, along with his brother Laxmana, used his meticulous battle skills to protect the saints and their yagnas. Rama never deviated from Vanavasa dharma. Even after defeating Ravana, Rama did not occupy Lanka territorially. He gave the kingdom of Lanka to Ravana's brother Vibhishana and returned to Ayodhya. Rama's purity of purpose transformed him as God Rama from King Rama in those fourteen years of exile. The virtues Rama had displayed and lived by during those challenging fourteen years made him stand out as 'Maryada Purushottam' Rama, which means the best among men. On the contrary, Ravana used his powers only to amass worldly pleasures, to kidnap Mata Sita, to grab Lanka and the Pushpaka Vimana from Kuber, etc.

According to scholars, the Ramayana is perhaps the oldest biography ever written.* But even after thousands of years,

_____

* The most conservative dating of the Ramayana, by D.K. Hari and Hema, is 5000 BCE. According to Dr Nilesh Oak, the Ramayana took place around 12,209 BCE. As it appears, in all probability, there is no other documented biography that has a reference older than that.

the characters of the Ramayana stand tall and teach us great values, and guide us towards the solutions to various real-life situations of today. Lord Brahma had correctly blessed Saint Valmiki, the great poet and author of the Ramayana, saying that 'as long as mountains stand on earth and rivers flow, the story of the Ramayana as narrated by Valmiki will remain current in all the worlds'.

This concludes the Yudha Kanda.

Life Lesson #25 for Families

Rama and Ravana both were brave, meritorious, scholarly and skilful. Rama used his virtues for the good of the mankind, while Ravana used his skills to boost his ego and amass worldly pleasures. Now you have to decide:

> **What do you want to be: Rama or Ravana?**

Family Scenario #25

Anshul is set to go to college now, away from parents in a different city. This college has one of best job-placement rates in the region, and so Anshul and his parents, Ram and Tara, have selected this college. The college has also given many successful entrepreneurs to the country. But it has one problem. It's known that students consume illegal substances at the hostel of this college. How should Ram and Tara guide Anshul for his independent life in college?

A) Anshul is a grown-up and can take his decisions himself
B) Ram and Tara should tell him the nuances of every aspect of the new college and hostel life, and allow Anshul to decide for himself
C) Ram or Tara, or both of them, should shift to the new city with Anshul, live with him and watch him closely

Guidance for Families from the Ramayana #25

Graduating to college after school is one of the major milestones in your child's life. Moving to a new city and living all by yourself add to the difficulty. Now Anshul has to take many small and big decisions himself: what to wear, what to eat, which courses to choose, what kind of friends to make, what kind of events and parties to attend, what career path to choose, etc. As parents, you can't prepare him for this through one or two discussions. Your parenting acumen, developed over years, will be put to the test now. Anshul's parents' conduct over the years in front of him has already created a framework for him to take decisions. It's best to teach and enable your children early in life to differentiate between good and bad, moral and immoral, dharmic and adharmic aspects, and between the Rama and the Ravana qualities within ourselves. There is a high probability that children brought up like this will take wise decisions for themselves when faced with real-life situations.

Your Favourite Character from the Yudha Kanda

In Yudha Kanda, we learnt about many characters of the Ramayana. First, list as many characters of the Yudha Kanda as you can. Then thoughtfully choose the character who inspires you the most. Also, share why and how that character inspires you. Different family members may have different favourite characters. You may want to note down your thoughts about your favourite character, click a picture and share on social media with the hashtag **#MyRamayana**.

_____

_____

_____

_____

_____

_____

_____

Kill the Ravana within You

At the end of the Yudha Kanda, let's take a moment to identify our 'Rama' and 'Ravana' qualities again. Then we should work to further strengthen our Rama qualities and get rid of our Ravana qualities. You have already done this exercise before in the book. Repeat the exercise one last time and reflect how it has helped you in self-realization. You may want to note down your answer, click a photo and share on social media with the hashtag **#MyRamayana**.

_____

_____

_____

_____

_____

_____

_____

_____

Yudha Kanda Crossword Puzzle

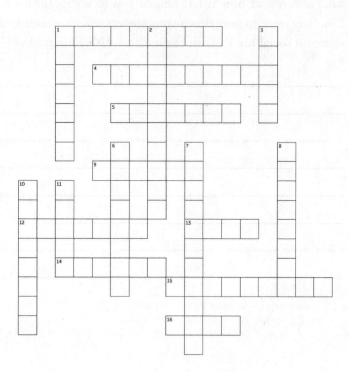

Across

1 Hanuman lifts the whole mountain to get this herb

4 An army was sent to wake him up from his sleep

5 The rakshasi who dreams the defeat of Ravana

9 He was also known as Lankeshwar

12 Also known as Indrajit

13 She was waiting for Rama at Ashoka Vatika

14 Celebrated to mark the return of Rama to Ayodhya

15 Wife of Ravana

16 Son of Vishwakarma and also the engineer of the Rama Setu

Down

1 He tells Rama not to trust Vibhishana

2 He was crowned the king after Ravana's death

3 The Rama Setu was built from Rameshwaram to reach _____

6 Ravana's maternal grandfather

7 The place where Rama built the Rama Setu

8 Celebrated for the demise of Ravana

10 The name of the bridge built from Rameshwaram to Lanka

11 He challenged all Ravana's courtiers to just move his leg

Find the answers on page 173

Answers to the Crossword Puzzles

Bala Kanda:
Across: 2. Laxmana 5. Maricha 9. Mithila 10. Sita 11. Rama 13. Kaikeyi
15. Bharata 17. Subahu 18. Bhagirath 21. Vishwamitra 22. Rishyasringa
23. Parashuram
Down: 1. Valmiki 3. Kausalya 4. Shatrughna 6. Sumitra 7. Tadaka 8. Urmila
12. Mandavi 14. Vasishtha 16. Shrutakriti 19. Ayodhya 20. Janaka

Ayodhya Kanda:
Across: 3. Dasharatha 5. Rama 6. Shravankumar 8. Guha 9. Sita 10. Bharata
12. Paduka 13. Laxmana 14. Dandaka
Down: 1. Kaikeyi 2. Chitrakoot 4. Sumantra 6. Sarayu 7. Manthara
10. Bharadwaj 11. Kausalya

Aranya Kanda:
Across: 2. Khar 4. Sita 8. Panchavati 9. South 10. Ravana
Down: 1. Rama 2. Kabandha 3. Surpanakha 5. Maricha 6. Laxmana 7. Dushan

Kishkinda Kanda:
Across: 1. Sampathi 4. Jambavan 6. Rishimukha 8. Bali 10. Hampi 15. Sugriva
16. Jatayu 17. Dundubhi 18. Laxmana
Down: 2. Hanuman 3. Shabari 5. Tara 6. Rama 7. South 9. Kishkinda 11. Angad
12. Jatayu 13. Sugriva 14. Ruma

Sundar Kanda:
Across: 4. Ravana 6. Indrajeet 9. Anjana 12. Ashokavatika 14. Vibhishana
15. Trikuta
Down: 1. Mainaka 2. Trijata 3. Lanka 5. Vishwakarma 8. Kesari 10. Hanuman
11. Lankini 13. Surasa

Yuddha Kanda:
Across: 1. Sanjivani 4. Kumbhkaran 5. Trijata 9. Ravana 12. Meghnad 13. Sita
14. Diwali 15. Mandodari 16. Nala
Down: 1. Sugriva 2. Vibhishana 3. Lanka 6. Malyavan 7. Rameshwaram
8. Dussehra 10. Ramasetu 11. Angad